PHILANTHROPY
Four Views

SOCIAL PHILOSOPHY & POLICY CENTER

PHILANTHROPY
Four Views

Robert Payton
Michael Novak
Brian O'Connell
Peter Dobkin Hall

transaction

Transaction Books
New Brunswick (USA) London (UK)

Published by the Social Philosophy and Policy Center
and by Transaction Publishers 1988

Library of Congress Cataloging-in-Publication Data

Payton, Robert L.
  Philanthropy: four views.

  1. Charities—United States. 2. Voluntarism—
United States. 3. United States—Social policy.
I. Title.
HV16.P39 1988   361.7'0973   87-36175
ISBN 0-912051-20-5
ISBN 0-912051-21-3 (pbk.)

The Center wishes to thank the Exxon Education Foundation for sponsoring the conference at which the essays
in this volume were originally presented.

Cover Design: Jacky Ahrens

TABLE OF CONTENTS

Introduction

CONTRIBUTORS

ROBERT L. PAYTON is Scholar-in-Residence in Philanthropic Studies at the University of Virginia. From 1977 to 1987, he was president of Exxon Education Foundation. He has also been president of Hofstra University and C.W. Post College, and vice chancellor for development and planning at Washington University in St. Louis. Mr. Payton served as United States Ambassador to the United Republic of Cameroon from 1967 - 1969. In 1984, he received the Distinguished Service to Education Award from the Council for Advancement and Support of Education. His book *Philanthropy* will be published by Macmillan in 1988.

MICHAEL NOVAK, theologian, author, and diplomat, is presently the visiting W. Harold and Martha Welch Professor of American Studies at the University of Notre Dame for the 1987 - 1988 academic year, and holds the George Frederick Jewett Chair in Religion and Public Policy at the American Enterprise Institute in Washington, DC, where he is Director of Social and Political Studies. He has served in various capacities under three presidential administrations and is the recipient of numerous awards for academic excellence and public service. Mr. Novak has also written over 20 books in the areas of philosophy, theology, politics, economics, and culture, and is author and editor of numerous monographs and over 200 articles and reviews. His writings have appeared in every major Western language, and in Bengali, Korean, and Japanese.

BRIAN O'CONNELL is the founding president of Independent Sector, a national coalition that now includes 650 foundations, corporations, and national voluntary organizations. Under his leadership, Independent Sector has become the country's leading advocate for our national traditions of giving and volunteering. Mr. O'Connell's career has been devoted to the promotion of private initiatives for the public good, and he has served with numerous organizations which address a wide variety of national concerns. Most of Mr. O'Connell's writing concerns voluntary action. His books include *Effective Leadership in Voluntary Organizations, The Board Member's Book, Our Organization, America's Voluntary Spirit,* and *Philanthropy in Action.*

PETER DOBKIN HALL is lecturer on Nonprofit Management at Yale's School of Organization and Management, Associate Research Scientist in the Program on Nonprofit Organizations, and a Visiting Professor in Wesleyan's Graduate Liberal Studies Program. His writings on business, philanthropy, community development, and the history of the family include *The Organization of American Culture, 1700 - 1900: Institutions, Elites, and the Origins of American Nationality* (1982). A history of the nonprofit sector, *The Private Culture*, will be published by Basic Books in 1988. He is currently completing a study of the social role of business corporations and their managers for Simon & Schuster.

INTRODUCTION

Philanthropy in the United States has embraced and supported an astounding variety of causes and institutions, and it has had an enormous impact on the character of our society. Every year, private citizens and private organizations contribute, literally, billions of dollars and billions of hours to relieve suffering, foster education and the arts, protect the environment, support scientific and other research efforts, and so forth. The activities of what has come to be known as the "independent sector"—the millions of individuals and organizations that contribute time and money to not-for-profit activities—are and always have been a major force in shaping the social institutions and public policies of the United States.

The important role that philanthropy and voluntarism plays in the United States has been widely recognized at least since Alexis de Tocqueville pointed it out in *Democracy in America* (1835). It is therefore somewhat surprising that the independent sector—in contrast to the private and public sectors—has received relatively little attention from social thinkers. Our understanding of the forces that have shaped American society is impoverished to the extent that the vital role of the "independent sector" has been neglected. The essays in this volume will enhance our appreciation of the importance of philanthropy in molding our society and in promoting innovation and social experimentation.

This connection between philanthropy and the foundations of American culture is the common theme that unites the essays which comprise this volume; the authors are concerned to elucidate the role that philanthropy plays in shaping our social institutions and in giving expression to the fundamental values of our culture. The essays represent the work of a historian (Peter Dobkin Hall), a social theorist (Michael Novak), and two practitioners (Robert Payton and Brian O'Connell) with wide-ranging experience at the forefront of the philanthropic world.

Robert Payton is Scholar in Residence in Philanthropic Studies at the University of Virginia and former president of the Exxon Education Foundation. In the latter role, he was actively engaged in fostering philanthropic support for education and encouraging scholarly attention to philanthropic

activities. In "Philanthropy in Action," he argues that the study of philanthropy has a clear and important place in a liberal education, and
especially in education in preparation for a life of public service. He defends
this thesis by providing numerous examples of contemporary philanthropic
activity and raising a number of questions about these examples. Many
of these questions, he argues, carry us well beyond mere technical competence into the realm of the philosophical. They are the questions of value,
purpose, and meaning that underlie virtually all human activity.

Michael Novak is George F. Jewett Scholar of the American Enterprise
Institute and a frequent commentator on the religious and philosophical
foundations of American culture. In "An Essay on 'Public' and 'Private',"
he argues that there is an essential connection between private philanthropic
institutions and the preservation of the limited state that guarantees individual freedom. When the state permits (and even encourages and promotes) private funding for a wide variety of philanthropic institutions, it
is in fact preserving itself as a *limited* state. For by encouraging philanthropy, the state delivers the protection and furtherance of the common
good into the hands of the citizens and thereby encourages the kind of
public-spiritedness that is essential to the preservation of freedom.

Brian O'Connell is President of Independent Sector, an organization
devoted to fostering and reporting on philanthropic activity in the United
States. In "Private Philanthropy and the Preservation of a Free and
Democratic Society," he points out that one of the most striking features
of the private or voluntary sector is its pluralism. The diversity of (often
incompatible) causes and institutions supported by private philanthropy
both reflects and preserves the political and cultural pluralism that is such
an important part of culture and political life in the United States.

Peter Dobkin Hall, a historian, is Associate Research Scientist of the
Institute for Social and Policy Studies at Yale University. In "Private Philanthropy and Public Policy: A Historical Appraisal," he charts the development of public health policy in Massachusetts and the role that voluntary
organizations played in this development. His conclusion is that the role
of private voluntary organizations was decisive in identifying the need for
and creating a public health policy.

There can be no doubt that, as faith in the ability of government to be
the sole guarantor of the public good wanes, the role of private voluntary
organizations will continue to expand. This points to a need for increased
attention to the principles and practices of philanthropy. The essays in this
volume are a contribution to this ongoing process of investigation, analysis,
and evaluation.

PHILANTHROPY IN ACTION

Robert Payton

A. What Is Philanthropy?

For the purposes of this essay, philanthropy will be defined as three related activities: voluntary service, voluntary association, and voluntary giving for public purposes. These activities and their interactions constitute what is variously known as the third sector, the independent sector, or the voluntary sector. The purposes of these activities include the traditional array, first outlined in the Statute of Charitable Uses in England almost 400 years ago: religion, education, health, the arts, and welfare.

These purposes can be roughly aggregated into two larger ideas: acts of mercy to relieve suffering, most commonly called charity and equivalent to relief in the realm of foreign aid; and acts of community to enhance the quality of life and to insure a better future—what is commonly called philanthropy and is the equivalent of development in foreign aid. It is in this sector that people mobilize themselves and others around moral rather than political or economic purposes, purposes which subordinate the uses of wealth and power to the common good.

What follows is a brief description and consideration of some of the ideas that represent the American philanthropic tradition in action.

B. The Range of Philanthropic Activity

1. The Ethiopian Famine Relief Effort

Few things have more effectively captured the public's sentiment in recent decades than the televised news reports about the Ethiopian famine first broadcast in the United States in 1984. The images dramatized suffering on a large scale among innocent people, particularly among defenseless children. The reports themselves indicated that literally millions of lives were in jeopardy, and that beyond immediate death by starvation there was also the prospect of large numbers of people mentally and physically maimed for life by lack of protein.

The surrounding conditions were shown to be almost unbelievably harsh: large numbers of people crowded into refugee camps—or, even worse, were unable to get into those camps at all. Thousands of people were reported to have died en route to the relief centers.

The political environment was also one of civil disorder. A government that described itself as Marxist—Leninist was engaged in drastic social and economic reform, including relocation of large numbers of people. A civil war between the central government in Addis Ababa and the secessionist rebel forces in Eritrea greatly complicated the situation: public resources were diverted to weapons and warfare rather than to relief efforts, and the central government attempted to block relief shipments to rebel territory as part of its military strategy.

The neighboring countries of the Sudan and Somalia, also suffering severely from the drought, were drawn into the Ethiopian crisis. Somalia has been engaged in sporadic warfare with the government of Ethiopia for some years; the two sides have exchanged international sponsors (the US and USSR). Sudan, divided by ethnic conflict north and south, proclaimed a policy of sanctuary for refugees fleeing from Ethiopia, even though resources to assist the refugees were critically needed by its own people.

The philanthropic constant in this situation might, for present purposes, be identified as the international relief community, which is led largely by American private voluntary organizations (PVOs) but also includes international agencies such as the UN refugee commission and other private agencies such as the French organization called Doctors Without Borders. The PVO community had warned of the impending crisis long before it became headline television news. A few American agencies were already in Ethiopia when the news story broke in the United States, even though the Ethiopian government's relations with the United States were at the lowest diplomatic level.

The Ethiopian crisis continues, but attention given to the crisis by the media has diminished sharply and shifted to other issues (most notably South Africa). What are some of the questions that have occurred in the course of the philanthropic response to the Ethiopian famine? Are they issues that might apply to similar crises elsewhere in the world?

- Is civil disorder the key? Drought in other African countries (most notably Botswana) has not resulted in suffering comparable to that in Ethiopia. To what extent should governments be held accountable for the suffering of their people in such circumstances? Does international relief ease the political burden on a bad government in Ethiopia?

- What is the true role of the famine relief effort? The sums raised, although historic in terms of voluntary giving for relief purposes, are a small fraction of the sums and supplies provided by governments. Is the role of private philanthropy that of consciousness-raising rather than the actual relief of suffering?

- To what extent should these problems be dealt with by voluntary giving? The scale of the financial need and the high levels of political action necessary to stabilize the country and the region exceed the grasp of voluntary action. Does voluntary giving obscure the need for more drastic and costly political action?

- On what basis can governments justify assistance to peoples where no significant political interest or benefit can be served? Our political "ally" in the region is Somalia; why should we help Somalia's principal enemy? Nor does Ethiopia have any importance to American economic interests; why invest a billion dollars in short-term refugee relief when the problem is likely to recur and when there will be no discernible or measurable benefit to the United States?

- Finally, what is the role of the news media? By extension, what are the appropriate uses of the media by entertainers acting as volunteers to raise money for famine relief? What impact will fund raising initiatives launched on behalf of Ethiopian famine relief have on large-scale fund raising for similar or even different purposes? Will international communication make international fund raising a new force in societies where private giving has been modest or nonexistent?

2. War and Revolution in Central America

The emergence of a Sandinista-dominated Marxist government out of the revolution against the Somoza government of Nicaragua has led to a strongly negative response from the government of the United States. The Reagan administration has given active support to rebel forces in opposition to the Sandinistas. At the same time, US policy has supported the government of El Salvador against rebels that reportedly receive support from Nicaragua. Similar civil and international military action, polarizing forces around extremes of left and right at the cost of moderate influences, is taking place in Honduras and Costa Rica. Peace initiatives have been sponsored by other governments (the Contradora group) as well as by the US (the so-called Kissinger commission), and by a wide range of private voluntary organizations.

To a much greater extent than in Ethiopia, religious groups have sought to influence public policy toward Central America—supporting Administration policy as well as opposing it. Voluntary action by church groups to provide "sanctuary" for refugees fleeing Central America has challenged immigration and refugee policy directly. Highly publicized legal action initiated against church groups has generated increased financial as well as moral support. Other religious groups that are pro-Administration have raised funds for humanitarian aid for the Nicaraguan rebels, funds that the Administration has been unable to extract from Congress. (The IRS classification of some of these nonprofit organizations is not made clear in newspaper reports.)

The essential question is the freedom of action claimed by and accorded to voluntary nonprofit organizations seeking to influence or change US foreign policy—by direct action outside the US.

- Can "humanitarian aid" be kept humanitarian in military situations? Are private contributions in fact fungible? Do they free up other funds for military purposes?

- Should boundaries be placed around the activities of church groups in foreign affairs? Is the separation of church and state jeopardized by the roles played by church groups in Central America?

- Does political action by churches and others undermine philanthropic behavior? How might we draw the line between politics and philanthropy?

3. Controlling Nuclear Weapons

This is the title of a new book by Robert Dahl, which examines the question in terms of the trade-off between "democracy and guardianship." At what point does a democracy yield its democratic processes to the decision of experts—when the consequences of error are catastrophic?

No issue is more familiar. Philosophers and others have engaged in extended discussions about it: the April 1985 issue of *Ethics,* for instance, was devoted to this topic. In terms of philanthropic action, the range of activities has spread across vast public rallies in Central Park on behalf of the nuclear freeze, teach-ins and student referenda at Brown University, the development and distribution of course materials and teacher guides by the Institute for World Order, and investment in academic research at a cluster of leading universities and research centers by the Carnegie Corporation.

Many have called for a massive effort to concentrate philanthropic resources and energies on this issue. The actual amount of funds allocated is probably small in the total scheme of philanthropic giving. The numbers of people enlisted in the debate, however, by educational and religious institutions, appears to run into the millions.

- To what extent should private voluntary organizations influence US nuclear policy? To what extent should US-based organizations attempt to influence the policies of other governments?

- To what extent is direct action of the kind most dramatically illustrated by Greenpeace justified within the framework of the philanthropic tradition?

- What is the role of the media in this issue? Are philanthropic organizations accorded different editorial treatment from that given to governmental and private economic points of view?

4. South Africa

Seldom has an issue become so intertwined among the three sectors. Private voluntary action has created effective pressures on business corporations and on intergovernmental relations. Religious organizations have again played a leading role, along with civil rights groups.

South Africa appears to have drawn attention away from the Ethiopian famine as the leading issue of African affairs pressing on the public consciousness. Voluntary efforts have become linked with political as well as religious and social groups within South Africa. The principal multinational corporation effort to improve the lot of South African blacks has been led by a black American clergyman, Leon Sullivan. Business corporations and philanthropic foundations have been the principal sponsors of black South Africans studying in the United States under a program managed by the Institute for International Education. The American Chamber of Commerce in South Africa was the focal point of a South African fund-raising effort, supplemented by funds from the US, to build a vocational school in Soweto. Colleges and universities with African studies and Afro-American studies programs have been the campus focal point for debate about the issue.

- What are the rights of private voluntary groups outside South Africa in supporting anti-apartheid protests that lead to violence and the deaths of South Africans?

- Is the strategy of disinvestment justified for religious organizations and educational institutions if the consequences are harmful to their own financial stability?

- Should philanthropic efforts in South Africa aim at long-term reform or short-term disruption?

- Are the philanthropic interventions in support of apartheid in South Africa (Jerry Falwell) or in opposition to it (almost everyone else) examples of American cultural imperialism? How do they differ?

5. Lincoln Center for the Performing Arts

The arts present the most permeable boundaries among the three sectors. Not only do for-profit and not-for-profit interests coexist with a variety of public agencies, initiatives that begin in one sector often mature in another. Foundation-supported artists make recordings with for-profit recording companies; tax-exempt theaters become the home of subsidized productions that eventually become highly profitable. Individuals are supported by sales of their work, by foundation grants, and by grants from public agencies such as the state arts councils and the National Endowment for the Arts. Lincoln Center is a familiar and symbolic hub of such activity, but many similar institutions have been established across the country.

- Should public funds be used to support activities that become profit-making?

- Should philanthropic funds, by definition not-for-profit, be permitted to result in private benefit? Should distinctions be drawn between artists, producers, and others in this regard?

- Does philanthropy subsidize elite culture with public money? Should public opinion be enlisted to validate or even guide the arts when public and philanthropic monies are involved?

- Should not-for-profit philanthropic enterprises be permitted to supplement their base income with resources earned by profit-making activity?

- Should access to the arts be free? Does the right to education have a cultural counterpart in the arts?

6. The Homeless

The homeless and derelict populations of large cities such as New York have increased substantially in recent years. Part of the cause appears to be reduced public funds for welfare; of perhaps even greater significance has been the decision to "mainstream" large numbers of the mentally retarded and others thought to be at risk in modern urban environments.

The homeless lay a heavy claim on the charitable conscience and on charitable funds. Their needs are linked to the religious traditions summarized in the New Testament: "For when I was hungry you gave me food; when thirsty, you gave me drink; when I was a stranger you took me into your home; when naked you clothed me; when I was ill you came to my help, when in prison you visited me." [Matthew 25:35-37, *New English Bible*]

A well-publicized controversy arose in New York City some years ago over the rights of religious organizations serving the homeless under city contracts. The Salvation Army and the Roman Catholic Church objected to requirements that, as contractors to the city, they sign statements affirming nondiscrimination in employment for homosexuals. The case appears to be a classic example of the conflict of two social goods.

- Do charitable organizations have special rights under the law that exempt them from legislation deemed to be in conflict with their ability to carry out their charitable objectives?

- Does charitable assistance to the poor lead to pauperization?

- Does charitable assistance to the poor relieve families of their obligations to family members who may be retarded or otherwise found "unacceptable" or too burdensome in the home?

- Should private agencies, especially those representing specific and strong religious convictions, be permitted to intervene in the lives of the homeless with financial support from public as well as private sources? Does the combination of efforts of New York City and the Salvation Army on behalf of the homeless violate the separation of church and state?

- Does public charity acting around rules of civil service develop workers in sufficient number and professional commitment to deal with the growing population of homeless, the mentally incompetent elderly, and those who are terminally ill? In the past, many if not most workers in these fields of service have been drawn to them by religious calling. Can a secular society inspire service of similar levels of self-sacrifice?

7. *Social Philosophy and Policy*

This last example deals with the thorny questions that grow out of reflection on the relationship of money and ideas, of means and influence. The conference for which this essay was originally written was an example of private funds being used to encourage the discussion and publication of the thoughts of philosophers and others on "Private Philanthropy and the Social Good." As this essay has attempted to demonstrate, the role of private philanthropy is far broader than fund raising and grant making, although it appears that most academics limit their reflection on the tradition to this single dimension. Some of the examples cited here—controlling nuclear weapons, the Central American conflict, the efforts to defeat apartheid in South Africa—call to mind the extensive interaction among campus-based academics, intellectuals in publishing and the media, and the alliances of secular intellectual with religious spiritual forces.

In some cases the philanthropic objectives to be served come into conflict with the sources of support. The risks fall on *all* participants in a philanthropic venture, not simply on those whose money is involved. More than money is in the game for the participants—status, prestige, reputation, and credibility are also at risk. This is often especially true in situations that are thought to be controversial. Risk is shared by corporations who may alienate shareholders and prospective investors, by churches divided into contending factions within local congregations, and by colleges and universities drawn into debates about external issues, debates that may antagonize otherwise sympathetic donors, parents, or prospective faculty members.

The larger public agenda advanced by a nonprofit organization may jeopardize the original and life-giving mission of the organization itself. Funds to supplant the monies lost to higher causes seem to be in short supply. The consequences of action may be ennobling and organizationally fatal at the same time.

The self-interest of donors is often lamented; less often heard is concern about the self-interest of recipients. Philosophers who deal with social and political philosophy deal routinely with explosive material, not only in the classroom but in their published work. Because some ideas of intellectual interest to philosophers are taboo in the larger society, it is often difficult for philosophers to find sponsors. (All too frequently, the threat to open philosophical discourse about issues that are taboo comes from within the academy rather than from outside. The most effective pressure on an academic may be that posed by hierarchical superiors in whom are vested powers over tenure decisions and promotion.)

Philosophers who affirm the standard of reason are also vulnerable to charges of bias, partisanship, and ideology when dealing with social issues. They may sometimes be rewarded for that same partisanship, of course, by pleasing those in the friendly camp, whether the camp is filled with

---

internal or external allies. But discourse suffers when partisanship triumphs, when interest—political, economic, or social—seems to outweigh rational argument.

It is difficult for the nonphilosophers to know how to cope with situations in which the experts—the philosophers—accuse one another of ideological distortion. In complex political situations, the facts are difficult to obtain as well as to interpret; the "data" are harder to control than in the scientific laboratory. It is much more difficult to reach agreement on public policy issues such as world hunger, political stability and peace in Central America, efforts to improve the prospects for world peace in the face of mass annihilation, and so on. Such issues raise difficult and often imprecise questions of the sort put forward above. Yet such issues cry out for the wisdom as well as the skills of those who devote their careers to thinking carefully about the social world and its values.

- To what extent does the world of philanthropy behave as a marketplace, where different styles and fashions and ideologies compete for support? To what extent do (and should) intellectuals compromise their intellectual objectives in order to win support?

- Is the marketplace of grants materially different from the campus competition for students or the publishing competition for readers? Should different standards of behavior be expected of the participants?

- How should philosophers be paid? ("Generously!" cried out one listener when I posed that question to an audience.) By earning their income from the sale of their work as teachers, writers, consultants, and lecturers? By subsidy from government agencies? By individual patronage? By subsidies in the form of grants from foundations and corporations? By some or all of the above?

- How should grant makers choose among the possible investments in social philosophy and policy? Should the goal be to encourage work on issues at the fringe of reflection and speculation, or should the goal concentrate on more immediate and practical objectives?

- What are the most successful models of the subsidy of philosophy? Which models appear to be most reliable over time?

- Is the philanthropic relationship corrupting in the realm of ideas as it is sometimes alleged to be in the realm of charity and almsgiving?

- Are philosophers more to be trusted in dealing with sensitive issues of social policy than are foundation executives, corporate executives, and agents of government?

C. Conclusion

1. Philosophical Inquiry

The intent of this essay is to cause trained and experienced students of philosophy to give clarity and direction to the philosophical discussion of philanthropy, as broadly defined here. What are the philosophical methods appropriate to addressing these particular questions?

Treated philosophically, the cases briefly defined above might prove to be the basis for extracting the ill-defined principles of philanthropy. They might help to bring to conscious reflection the inconsistencies, paradoxes, and contradictions between philanthropic behavior in different settings.

How do the specific questions reveal larger social issues? For example, to what extent may they be used to consider in concrete terms some of the underlying trade-offs between the short term and long term? They force us, I believe, to consider the political dimension of philanthropic action— the gray area between public education and consciousness-raising, for example, and lobbying. How might we begin to formulate a defensible distinction between philanthropy intended to improve the quality of life in the community and political action that proclaims the same high purpose?

Moving from specific examples of philanthropy in action (more fully and carefully delineated than they are sketched out here, of course), we can begin to identify the characteristics of voluntary action. It would seem from the cases themselves that there is a greater readiness for interaction among the not-for-profit, for-profit, and governmental sectors during times of crisis than at times that are more normal. Such observations might, in turn, eventually carry us to higher levels of philosophical discourse: for example, to what extent is the philanthropic dimension determinative of the social order? To what extent does philanthropy reveal the nature of society?

2. Philanthropy in Education

The emphasis of this essay has been on the contribution to social philosophy and policy that might result from a better understanding of philanthropy in action. The study of philanthropy should be considered in the framework of education as well as that of research, policy, and practice. How should philanthropy be approached in teaching? The illustrations of philanthropy in action that make up the second part of this essay appear as grist for most of the disciplinary mills of the humanities and social sciences. I have proposed that we deal with their philanthropic dimension explicitly.

What are the principles of philanthropy, and how are they taught and learned? By systematic investigation in formal academic study, or by experience and the guidance of mentors in the context of voluntary service? What are the appropriate methods of philanthropy, the methods that best protect the integrity of philanthropic relationship? Is the model of nonprofit organization effective? Can voluntary initiative carry the burden of important social needs, of advancing the spheres of distributive justice? Must charity be coerced?

These questions may be appropriate to liberal education in preparation for a life of public service. They may be of considerable consequence in the general education of young Americans as citizens. They are questions, however, that go well beyond technical competence. Technical competence is required of young people these days, as is competence in verbal and mathematical expression and reasoning, and the useful skills of dealing with others. The latter skills are of special importance in situations where responses are not obligatory and where self-interest is often unclear. These are common situations when people come together for public purposes.

Questions of value, purpose, morality, and meaning are raised by exploration of philanthropy in action. They are also questions of the kind that most people still think of as philosophical questions. Does philanthropy then have a proper place in the philosophical curriculum?

AN ESSAY ON "PUBLIC" AND "PRIVATE"

Michael Novak

One of the most overlooked characteristics of the free society is the principle that it is not necessary—it is even dangerous—to serve public needs soley through the state. Put otherwise, this principle holds that as far as possible even public needs should be met freely. Individual freedom is not inconsistent with public-spiritedness. On the contrary, in a free society, the individual must be conceived to be not the "possessive individual," but the "public-spirited individual." For as air is to lungs, so is public spiritedness to the maintenance of freedom.

1. American Originality

True enough, many public needs are well served by the state, through the use of the taxing power. The range of public services is large. In a continental and highly mobile society such as that of the United States, many individuals find themselves in neighborhoods in which they are hardly known to others. In extremity, some may have need of assistance when no one nearby is aware of their need. For such reasons, it has seemed good to the American people to construct a national, largely state-directed "safety net." Similarly, National Institutes of Health have been built—perhaps the most distinguished centers of medical research in the history of medicine. A National Endowment for the Arts, and another for the Humanities—and even a National Endowment for Democracy, to assist democratic movements abroad—have been established. In principle, it is altogether proper for the government of the United States "to promote the general welfare" through state agencies of these sorts, and many others.

Still, to attend to public needs solely through the state would have several drawbacks. One is that there is the unavoidable aspect of coercion; tax monies must be raised through the full majesty of punitive law. Another is that the definition of public need is rendered at least somewhat monolithic: those needs are met through the law that are defined in law. The citizenry as a whole, or in its many parts, may be aware of many other needs emerging among a pluralistic and geographically widely dispersed population that current law overlooks.

Thus, the principle that public needs should *also* be met through the vigilance and organizing skills of free citizens has seemed to be an indispensable principle of the fully free society. As John Gardner has said: "Perhaps the most striking feature of the [philanthropic] sector is its relative freedom from constraints and its resulting pluralism. Within the bounds of the law, all kinds of people can pursue any idea or program they wish."[1] Unlike aid through the state, any free group of citizens need not await the formation of the large constituency necessary for governmental action. The group may meet the public needs that it discerns, acting expeditiously to meet them.

Indeed, one of the secrets of the American order is its originality in solving the question of how to involve its citizens in the commonweal. What in France is accomplished through the state and in Britain through the aristocracy, Alexis de Tocqueville writes, is in America accomplished through its own citizens in voluntary associations. Americans, he marvels, do almost *everything* through their own associations:

> Americans of all ages, all stations in life, and all types of dispositons are forever forming associations. There are not only commercial and industrial associations in which all take part, but others of a thousand different types—religious, moral, serious, futile, very general and very limited, immensely large and very minute. Americans combine to give fetes, found seminaries, build churches, distribute books, and send missionaries to the antipodes. Hospitals, prisons, and schools take shape in that way. Finally, if they want to proclaim a truth or propagate some feeling by the encouragement of a great example, they form an association. In every case, at the head of any new undertaking, where in France you would find the government or in England some territorial magnate, in the United States you are sure to find an association.[2]

This new habit of association is an original and powerful principle of the common good. Tocqueville further identifies the *law of association* as a new first principle of the social order:

> Among laws controlling human societies there is one more precise and clearer, it seems to me, than all the others. If men are to remain civilized or to become civilized, the art of association must develop and improve among them at the same speed as equality of conditions spreads.[3]

Consider the originality of this principle. In order nations, care for the common good is typically left to the state. "Public" is allowed to mean "state," "common," "caring." "Private" is limited to meaning "self-interested." But in the light of American reality, that is an absurd restriction of terms.

2. The Case of Sweden

A vivid counterexample may be observed in Sweden. Denis P. Doyle describes the situation: The Swedish Secretariat for Futures Studies (SFS), the Swedish equivalent to a top U.S. presidential commission, recently issued a crucial report, "Care and Welfare at the Crossroads." Care and welfare in Sweden are entirely in the hands of the state. "Even the church is financed by the government, and the creation of even one non-profit philanthropic organization would be a quantum jump."[4]

Studying economic trends, long-term demographics, and tastes and preferences for care, the SFS concludes that by the year 2000 Sweden simply will not be able to meet the social bills the state has already contracted. Fourteen percent of Swedish GNP is committed to governmental care. The state's caring professionals exact high salaries. By 2000, about 20 percent of GNP will be committed. The tax burden will be staggering. Already 50 percent of GNP goes into taxes. The SFS projects that by the year 2000 more than 60 percent will be required.

Since it is "unacceptable" to Swedes to reduce either the quantity or the quality of care, or to freeze the salaries of care providers, the SFS has finally been *obliged* to turn to the private sector. How can it do so, with no independent private sector to turn to? As Doyle puts it, "The answer is simplicity itself: Compel voluntarism."[5] The SFS recommends that the Swedish government not only levy *taxes* but also begin to levy *time*. Every Swede aged 19 to 65, no exceptions, will be compelled to donate 4 to 6 hours a week to caring for others. The state will now re-create the private sector by state coercion. Thus is the system of forced labor reinstalled.

3. "Public" and "Private"

Few Americans accept as the map of reality the map provided by socialist thought (democratic socialist or social democrat), but those few are influential, not least among philosophers. Their categories of thought influence much that is written in the daily press. Thus, one often finds the following connotative chains linked to the two central words of social policy, "public" and "private." I think the following chart reflects much current usage.

PUBLIC	PRIVATE
Common good	Self-interest
Community	Individual
Civic responsibility	Self-centered
Compassion	Greed
"Family"	Darwinism
Caring	Cold, calculating
Other-regarding	Self-regarding
Generosity to the needy	Market-oriented
People	Profits

If one thinks about American reality, however, these neat ideological categories fall apart. In 1980, for example, U.S. foundations, corporations, and individuals contributed some $48 billion for charitable purposes. Independent Sector, an association that tries to keep track of private giving, estimates that in addition volunteers contributed labor whose cash value was about $65 billion. These figures from 1980 (totaling $113 billion) exceed by $23 billion the $90 billion in noncash benefits given by the federal government to the poor in 1980. Further, this $90 billion is nearly three times as much as would have been needed simply to give every poor nonfarm family of four enough cash to lift them above the official poverty line for 1980.

Think of it this way. The number of the poor in 1980 was 29.3 million. Divided—as a thought experiment—into families of four, this sum is the equivalent of 7.3 million such families. The official poverty line for a nonfarm family of four in 1980 was $8,414. The total sum needed "from scratch" to give each of these 7.3 million families a full $8,414 in 1980 would have been $61.4 billion. But one does not need to begin "from scratch." The poor already earn about half the sum necessary to lift all of them out of poverty. In 1980, therefore, the poor needed approximately an additional $30 billion of income to place above the poverty line.

To be sure, most private charitable giving in 1980 did not go directly to the poor. Most went to cancer research, community action projects, symphonies, universities, the churches, and many other instruments of the common good. Still, the sum of money voluntarily contributed considerably exceeded the $90 billion invested by the federal government in noncash benefits in 1980 for medicare, medicaid, food stamps, housing assistance, and the like.

The economist Walter Williams cites figures showing that 80 percent of privately contributed funds in all of human history have been donated by American citizens. In few nations are the tax laws, the habits of the population, the general ethos, and the institutional traditions of private generosity so favorable to private giving. For such reasons, this nation rightly prides itself upon the *public-spiritedness* of the *private* sector.

In America, "private" in part *means* "public-spirited." Citizens meet their civic responsibilities toward the public welfare and the common good without doing so solely through the state. The common good is considered to be served at least as well by the private sector as by the public sector, and in some ways better served.

Of course, the American people are also exceedingly generous in the caring they are willing to exercise through the state. Not counting state or private contributions to the welfare of their fellow citizens, Americans in 1984 assigned $439 billion for expenditures through the federal government alone for "human resources." These federal expenditures went for social security and medicare ($240 billion); health ($31 billion); noncash income security ($113 billion); education, training, and employment ($29 billion); and veterans benefits and services ($26 billion).[6]

No previous generation in American history has contributed such large sums, through the federal government, for welfare and caring. Many question how effective this spending has been. What no one can deny is the generous impulse behind it.

In short, Americans are virtually unique among the peoples of the world in recognizing *two* channels for attending to their civic responsibilities. Americans care for the needy in their midst and seek to provide a very broad range of public goods and services in two ways. They do so both through the public sector (the state), by means of tax-supported state programs, and through the private sector, by means of voluntary contributions of money, labor, and time.

A close examination of how Americans use the language of "public" and "private" is, therefore, long overdue. Does "public" always mean compassionate? Must "private" always be linked to "individualistic"? In American practice, private sector activities are often highly organized, social, and even bureaucratic. The realm of the social is recognized to be far larger than the realm of the state. Many "public" goods and services are provided by private organizations. The time is ripe for reconsideration. In addition, American politics is at a new crossroads.

4. The New Situation

Looking toward the last fifteen years of the twentieth century, we face a remarkable opportunity in American political philosophy. On all sides, there is widespread dissatisfaction with prevailing habits of mind. One hears democratic socialists glumly query each other, "What's left?" One hears liberals speak of the need for "new ideas," not simply programmatic ideas but foundational ideas. One hears conservatives argue that the most conspicuous failure of conservatism lies in not developing its own social vision. New facts, a new situation, and new currents of reflection foretell a new beginning.

In the past, much of political philosophy has been written around the two novel poles of modernity: the individual and the state. On the whole, the right, faced with a problem, has turned for its solution to the individual, while the left, faced with a problem, has turned to the state. Roughly speaking, since the New Deal, American conservatives have gloried rhetorically in "the individual"; American liberals have gloried in "The Great Society." It is not too far from the truth to write, in the rough language of generalization, that the Republican Party has failed to develop a social vision, let alone a social program, both because of its antipathy to the state and because of its own concerns for the individual, whereas the Democratic Party has been, par excellence, the party of social vision and social programs. Yet today, some fifty years after the New Deal, reassessments are taking place in both camps. Both on the left and the right, experience has obliged thoughtful persons to rethink their premises.

On the right, three lessons have been assimilated. First, conservatives have come to realize that, in a society such as ours, a significant number of individuals cannot be self-sufficient and thus have a legitimate need for governmental assistance. A conservative consensus has emerged about the legitimacy of a "safety net." Second, conservatives have gained considerable political power and, with it, new responsibilities. They know that they must now demonstrate unaccustomed skills both in social philosophy and in social management. Third, in part through the infusion of neoconservative intellectuals (that is, former progressives who have become critical of progressivism), in part through the thoughtfulness and ambition of a new breed of young conservatives, the conservative movement has grasped the importance of the idea of the future. They see that they must have a vision of the shape of a society yet to be built. Consequently, conservatives have been developing a fresh set of ideas about social philosophy and social programs. The term "social invention" is in the air. Ambition is father to thought.

On the left, many intent on loyalty to the liberal vision have also been honest in facing three deficiencies in the liberal practice of the past fifty years. The virtually automatic support that liberals have given to new government programs has been chastened. Many liberals now recognize that such programs are costly, plagued by a certain impersonality and bureaucratization, and, to a considerable extent, often counterproductive. They see, in a word, that such programs necessarily have many unintended consequences, sometimes of an ironic and damaging sort. Aid that makes its recipients dependent, for example, falls short of liberal ideals of dignity and autonomy. Further, such aid sometimes becomes an incentive to further increases in the very pathology it was intended to ameliorate. The discussion of "perverse incentives" has become commonplace.

One can summarize these changes on the right and on the left in this way: philosophically, the idea of "society" is now seen to be far larger than the twin poles of the conventional discussion, the "individual" and the "state." Human beings are social animals (political animals, as Aristotle put it), were such before the advent of the modern state, and remain such within it. Against the modern right, this lesson illuminates how even the highly developed, autonomous individual is the fruit of a *social* history, of specific social institutions, and indeed of a famlily life of a historically particular kind. Against the modern left, this lesson illuminates how the social nature of human life can be expressed through many other agencies besides the state, and through many other spheres of life besides the political.

In a sense, then, both from the left and from the right, modern political philosophy is being turned towards the analysis of a zone much neglected in the received literature, the zone of social living *in between* (as it were) the pole of the autonomous individual, on the one side, and the state or large collective, on the other.

Human beings live, move, and have their being in many social institutions smaller than, or different from, the state. Among these, the preeminent institution is the family. There are also the ethnic or cultural group; religious institutions; associations, corporations, or voluntary groups of many kinds; educational institutions; unions; cultural organizations; committees; and many other social forms. To paraphrase Oscar Wilde, the trouble with free societies is that they inspire many committees.

According to one literary convention, Americans are described as individualists, loners, Marlboro men, even "cowboys." A contrary convention describes them as compulsive joiners, organization men (and women), a lonely crowd. It is not easy to find such conventions actually descriptive of the Americans one knows in person, or of American life as it is lived. Still, without settling upon an exact description of American life that is critical of existing conventional wisdom, it is only fair to call attention to the thick texture of American social life, the texture that draws millions of us out of isolation and into many different sorts of social activity. A quick examination of conscience reveals how many associations each of us actually belongs to—how many meetings each of us actually attends.

In trying to imagine a social framework for meeting public needs, then, we find a great many social institutions already in existence to which philosophical thought has given surprisingly little attention: the multiplicity of social institutions that mediate between the individual and the state. If conservatives are ready to admit that the individual alone is not always sufficient, and if liberals are ready to admit that not all the social goods that need to be achieved can be achieved throught the state, perhaps there can be a new beginning in the philosophy of social policy, through sustained reflections upon *mediating institutions*. If we begin with the premise that there are many individuals in need of social assistance, we need not conclude that the only or the best way of meeting these social needs is through the state. Many existing social institutions might be further cultivated, strengthened, and directed toward meeting social needs. This new premise of social philosophy—the existence and the functioning of mediating institutions—sheds new light upon practical approaches to social policy.

For example, of intact married-couple families in 1984, only 6.9 percent were below the poverty line. Helping families to stay together does seem to be an effective way to keep people out of poverty. Here, a fresh practical possibility emerges. Adjustments in the tax law could be of considerable assistance to low-income families. As matters stand, poverty figures reflect income before taxes; after taxes, poverty bites even harder. New tax proposals before the Congress late in 1985 would abolish federal income tax obligations for families in poverty and for some income level (not yet finalized) close to 25 percent above the poverty line. In addition, the tax exemption for dependents would be significantly raised—President Reagan has requested $2000 per dependent, up from the current $1000—for all income earners but the most affluent. These two measures, if both became law together, would be of significant financial help to families among the poor and the near-poor. These measures might not effect the official pretax poverty figures, but they would certainly allow needy families to keep more of their own earnings. These measures might also have important and favorable incentive effects.

These practical ideas were arrived at by a small number of White House aides focusing on how to ease the situation of poor families. The aim of these aides was not to create some new government agency but, rather, to discern what government could do to strengthen an already existing social institution of considerable moment in the struggle against poverty, the family. Although these reformers at first faced stiff opposition from those worried chiefly about deficits—and, therefore, about the loss of tax revenues—the reformers carried the day by the strength of the new philosophical premise of mediating structures. They made four arguments. Help families, they said, as a means of combating poverty; at the very least, relax the demands of government upon already hard-pressed families. It makes no sense, they further pointed out, to tax the poor with one hand, while offering them federal benefits with another. Third, they pointed out that families provide crucial social benefits, which in the absence of families are extremely difficult for government to provide: the inculcation of good habits of study, work, moral concern, and so forth. And it makes good social sense to strengthen families, they argued, not, in this case, by direct intervention but by *withdrawing* the intervention of the long arm of taxation.

Public policy cries out for extending this new mode of analysis (not necessarily connected with tax policy) into other areas of public need. The main point is to examine the strengths and needs of existing social institutions, and to discern ways in which government might help them to achieve their own proper social roles—or at least cease *hurting* them. As with most social institutions, moreover, such mediating institutions have a nearly protean character and an amazing flexibility, enabling them to adapt to new circumstances, to meet newly emerging needs, and to accept new challenges. The strength of a free society lies in the strength of its mediating social institutions precisely because of their capacity to adapt to the open-endedness of liberty itself.

5. Three Contributions of the Private Sector

If the foregoing analysis had merit, the common good can *only* be met through the joint efforts of the state and the private sector. In the new situation, both state and private efforts are needed in order to actualize the latent energies of the citizenry. The resources to be drawn upon are threefold: monetary, perceptual and analytical, and expertise and enterprise. A few comments on each are in order.

(1) *Monetary.* Most social activities cost money: to rent an office, install telephones, hire places for meetings, pay for lunches, employ specialists, create mailing lists, or maintain networks of information, and so forth. One of the advantages of having private sources of funding is flexibility. The expenditure of government funds is necessarily restricted and subject to time-consuming processes of accountability, in the light of criteria often far removed from local circumstances. Further, reliance on governmental funds alone is subject to the vicissitudes and daily demands of politics; what government giveth, government can take away. Long-term commitments from activists depend on commitments from many others; a certain local cohesion, dedication, and proof of long-term financial support are psychological necessities. Thus, one sees around the nation today the formation of many local foundations and local organizing groups tightly focused on problems of significant concern to existing communities. The reality of local concern generates monetary commitment. Sustained private efforts on the national level also require long-term monetary commitment.

(2) *Perceptual and analytical.* Perhaps the single greatest advantage of the American tradition of private-sector concern for the public good is that it broadens the range of creative intellects engaged with public problems. This multiplication of potential sources of perspective, insight, and sound practical judgment increases the probability of creative solutions. By contrast, in nations obliged to rely solely upon government officials, the potential sources of perception and analysis are significantly narrower. Put otherwise, one of the greatest assets of any society is its operative pool of social intelligence. The larger the number of persons drawn into that pool and made to concentrate their intellects upon practical solutions to public perplexities, the greater the probabilities of effective insight. What one person does not perceive, another may. A pattern of analysis deeply entrenched in the conventional wisdom may strike a newcomer to the question as insufficient. A fresh way of analyzing the data may emerge. Moreover, the multiplication of cadres of citizens concerned about social problems enhances the potential variety of perspectives, ways of thinking, and criteria of judgment. If the competition of ideas is essential to the free society, then the maintenance of many private centers of inquiry, each in competition with the others, raises the probability that deficiencies in the current conventional wisdom will be detected and overcome.

The free society, then, depends not only upon the separation of systems (the separation of the institutions of conscience, ideas, and information from the political system—the state—and the further separation of the economic system, by some significant degree, from the state), and not only upon the separation of powers within the state (executive, legislative, and judicial). It also depends upon a pluralism of institutions of perception and analysis. For one of the most crucial constitutive elements of the public good is the public fund of social intelligence, incarnated in as large as possible a pool of intelligent and reasoning citizens.

This fund of social intelligence, in turn, depends today upon an active pluralism of neutrally critical and self-critical centers of inquiry of a more or less specialized and professionalized sort. So many skills and hard-earned bodies of experience are required by social intelligence, if it is to function in some reasonable relation to reality, that individual persons necessarily depend upon the honed skills and patiently acquired practical wisdom of many colleagues. This requirement imposes the happy necessity both of colleagueship and of some degree of professionalization in highly organized centers of inquiry. There is so much to be known, and there are so many disparate materials to be taken account of, that one person alone is typically no match for the complexity of modern societies. For this reason, participation in organized centers of professional inquiry is immensely helpful to the individual talent, if the latter is to function knowledgeably and well. Simultaneously, so as not to become captive to one school of thought alone, the free society requires many such centers, pluralistic in their differences from one another.

Historically, great centers of private philanthropy have played a socially creative role precisely in developing centers of inquiry designed to add to existing social intelligence. Further, they have often pioneered in the development of new forms of social expertise, e.g., in the advancement of preventive health through the gathering of statistics, through (at first widely resisted) programs of inoculation and vaccination, through the professionalization of medicine, and through the funding of great centers of medical research. Similarly, private philanthropy has often given impetus to research and training in many other pioneering social professions, including social work, public administration, and modern corporate management. The fact that private philanthropy did not need to wait for the political acceptability of its initiatives, but could act decisively in uncharted areas, was of decisive importance to the promotion of the general welfare. New perceptions of need and new methods of analysis could thereby be institutionalized *through* private sources but *for* public betterment.

(3) *Expertise and Enterprise.* Since social problems do not always solve themselves, it is often indispensable that someone exhibit the necessary enterprise, attempt to discover and to systematize the requisite expertise, and begin transferring the newly acquired social intelligence to others. While we speak properly of *social* intelligence, both in the sense that among the proposed beneficiaries thereof is society at large, and also in the further sense that such intelligence must come to be embodied in many persons throughout society, it is nonetheless true that fresh intelligence first flashes forth in one mind alone or among a small band of colleagues.

Human intelligence functions through the imagination, in close contact with the concrete. New insights arise in one particular mind at a time, even if in a social setting. These insights, often at first inarticulate, then need to be expressed in terms that are easily communicated to others (of different experience, background, and disposition). Some concrete human person, therefore, must *make an effort* to discover new understandings, and many further efforts to communicate these understandings. That is why one cannot neglect the factor of *enterprise*. Someone must originate and carry through the necessary effort, usually a sustained one, and usually one that reveals its secrets to others only in proportion as they themselves make comparable efforts to gain the desired understanding. That is why one cannot neglect the factor of social discipline or *expertise*. Social intelligence, for most of us most of the time, yields only to disciplined effort; its acquisition is far from effortless.

Here too, then, private philanthropy has been midwife to a considerable proportion of acquired social intelligence in the United States. In order to free a significant number of persons from the demands of daily living, private philanthropy has endowed chairs of research, centers of new knowledge, and institutions for the communication of expert knowledge. Allowing some to dedicate sustained efforts to the acquisition and the transmission of new social intelligence, such philanthropy has significantly contributed to the common good.

6. Rethinking the National Community

Nonetheless, there is a tendency for many intellectuals in the United States, as I suggested in the early part of this essay, to identify the public good with the works of the state, and to link the private sector solely to private interests. How can this frame of mind persist in the face of so much evidence to the contrary? Behind it, I think, lies an ancient instinct, which even has the force (in this case misleading) of common sense. Intuitively, in wish and in desire, one would truly like to think of the human community as united, organic, and all-embracing. One would like such a community to stand as an alternative to individual "alienation." One would like to think the human community at peace, brother to brother, sister to sister, united in great and noble purposes. Most images of Heaven are of this sort, whether the Heaven of various major religions, the Lost Paradise of primeval beginnings, or the Paradise, ever up ahead, of socialism on earth. The underlying idea, so deep that it is seldom rendered articulate, is that in such a Heaven-on-earth, each human person could pursue *simultaneously* both what maximizes his or her own individuality and also what maximizes the common good of all. This vision is quasi-religious. It is the dream of human solidarity. It is certainly a noble social vision.

Applied to politics, this vision finds expression in the politics of the Great Community. (Lyndon Johnson's Great Society drew upon the historic potency of this dream.) Here, public officials would have at heart solely the public good, and individual citizens would be ennobled by a common public enterprise. Any falling off from this vision would be defined as "selfishness," "possessive individualism," "greed," or even social "Darwinism." Caring about others, compassion, "giving a damn," reaching out to the poor and the oppressed, submerging the self in the demands of a public-spirited conscience and in sensitivity to the needs of others, would characterize, if not everybody, then at least the new "constituency of conscience," the historical carrier of the democratic socialist vision. Like Franklin Delano Roosevelt, the partisans of such a politics would establish the moral preeminence of the National Community, its leadership exercised by elected representatives. The whole of the United States would come to be seen as a nation with the soul of a church: a nation of committed, caring, compassionate, and sensitive citizens of conscience.

So long as the guardians of this vision seemed to serve the common good, this vision had great persuasive power among the largely Christian, Jewish, and humanistic citizenry of the United States. As events unfolded, however, this vision seemed more and more to be serving the interests of a particular elite: the limousine liberals, the cheese and chablis set, the suburban SDS, and the like. In addition, many of its specific diagnoses of American society seemed to many citizens wildly out of touch with undeniable realities. The vision fragmented.

The error in this generic vision of the left, as I believe it may be fairly designated, lay in confusing a secular religion, or at least a moral vision, with politics. It attempted to attach to political processes and institutions the full majesty of religious and moral transcendence. A premature reaching for salvation in this world, it tried to realize Heaven on earth. Real politics, by contrast, must cope with the human community and human beings as we are: divided, of discordant ideals and purposes, carrying vastly different conceptions of reality, partly blinded by egotism and passion, self-flattering and self-deceiving, neither angels nor brutes. The purpose of politics is not to fashion Heaven on earth, for the degree of communal solidarity politics can hope to bring about is painfully modest. In the world as it is, e.g., progressives do not really believe that they are in "solidarity" with conservatives, reactionaries, and rightists, bare tolerance is difficult enough.

The fractiousness of human communities is, indeed, a given of politics. One can hope to bring about a certain level of civility and cooperation, and one can even work to achieve an era of notable fellowship and good feeling. But solidarity is too much to ask of a genuinely pluralistic people whose individual philosophies of life are in considerable disharmony. Certainly, one cannot without destroying liberty itself bring about solidarity *through the coercive power of the state.*

That is why the United States, after some fifty years of movement in the direction of the Great Community, stands at a new beginning. The Great Community has in practice come to seem utopian. As such, and ironically, it may even be destructive of such community as a free nation needs. Those coerced by majorities into policies they abhor will rebel. The "balkanization" of the discontent—such as was widely reported in the mid-1970s—led in fact to the coalescing of a new majority.

7. Realism and Modesty

Where, then, do we stand? The nation seems to be seeking a new image to express its own identity. One Great Community it is not, and cannot be. Yet it can be a Community of Communities, ruled by civility and sensible argument, cooperative, alive with dissent and new initiatives, active in millions of local, regional, and national associations. Civility, not solidarity, can be its ruling unitive passion. Agreeing to disagree—and agreeing, further, to offer public argument even for each party's deepest reasons for disagreement—can be the dominant motif of its public discourse. The American people are not a homogeneous people. Although one, we are a pluralistic people. There is pride in this American experiment in pluralistic unity. The ideal of unity without solidarity may be the most original social experiment in history.

Moreover, government itself is once again being demystified. We do not elect public officials to be our archbishops or the chaplains of our souls. We do not engage in politics to find salvation, whether here or hereafter. Nor are public officials the chief vessels of our many moral visions. On the contrary, as Americans conceive it, the purpose of government is "to secure our rights, to provide for the common defense, to ensure justice, to attain domestic tranquility, to promote the general welfare, and to transmit the blessings of liberty to our posterity." These alone are a sufficiently large order. The purpose of government is not to secure Heaven on earth, but to provide a reasonable framework of order within which a community of free persons can pursue their deeply cherished visions of justice in tolerable amity.

Modesty is an indispensable characteristic of the limited governments of free peoples. In order to pursue the common good, therefore, we must also have active and potent agencies outside government. It is the task of private giving and private philanthropy—both of them oriented toward the public good—to nourish these agencies. I do not see how a free society can long survive without private giving and private philanthropy. How else will homogenization be avoided? How else will the fund of social intelligence be constantly renewed from competitive and dissident sources? How else will the thousand coercions of the would-be beneficent state, with their encroachments on the minutest details of daily life, be submitted to analysis, restraint, check, and the opening of alternative avenues of free life? Those who give the public fund of social intelligence solely into the hands of the state surrender too much of their liberty.

For this reason, the state is not merely tolerant when it permits, in fact encourages and promotes, the development of private funding for a vast panoply of philanthropic institutions. Such a state protects itself from ceasing to be a limited state. Nor is such self-restraint on the part of the limited state an act of generosity. It is, on the contrary, an act of self-preservation. If it did otherwise, it would strip away its own limits and become something else altogether.

When the limited state allows private persons to make private bequests of the substance they have earned, and thus to launch their purposes into the stream of future history, such a state declares in an unmistakable way that its own ambition does not exceed its own limited purposes, and that the state is not coterminous with society. It recognizes in practice that society is far larger in its sweep than the limited state, and that even the public good, the commonweal, exceeds by immense stretches the limited domain of the state. In a free society, the public good is in the keeping of all its citizens, well beyond the limited public order that it is the sworn duty of the state to uphold. As the rights of citizens are prior to the state, so also is their conception of, and their pursuit of, the common good. For the right to pursue their own happiness is not merely a privatized right. It includes the right to pursue their own conception of the public good, within which their personal good finds its proper place.

8. Summary

In summary, experience has taught the people of the United States that government, even good government with all its blessings, is less than an adequate instrument of the public good. To attain the public good in its fullness, many more agencies than those of the state must be fully and freely engaged.

After the ravages of recent decades, the people of the United States are in need of a renewed philosophy of the public good. In that philosophy, the private sources of monetary backing, perception and analysis, and expertise and enterprise—sources of social vitality that spring from the free acts of free citizens, infused with the public-spiritedness that is one of this nation's traditional and singular virtues—have an honored and indispensable place.

NOTES

[1]John Gardner, Address to Charter Meeting of Independent Sector, March 5, 1980.

[2]Alexis de Tocqueville, *Democracy in America*, ed. J.P. Mayer and Max Lerner, trans. George Lawrence (New York: Harper & Row, 1966), p. 485.

[3]*ibid.*, p. 488.

[4]Denis P. Doyle, *Wall Street Journal*, August 27, 1985.

[5]*ibid.*

[6]U.S. Bureau of the Census. *Statistical Abstract of the United States: 1985*. 105th ed. Washington, D.C.: U.S. Bureau of the Census, 1984. Table no. 492.

PRIVATE PHILANTHROPY AND THE PRESERVATION OF A FREE AND DEMOCRATIC SOCIETY

Brian O'Connell

The United States is the longest-lived democracy in the history of the world. This democracy has provided almost all of us with greater freedom and opportunity than any nation of human beings has ever known. Among the crucial factors that foster and preserve that democracy and those freedoms are active citizenship and personal community service.

In any attempt to sort out the roles and responsibilities of citizenship, it is important to start with the basic values of American society:

—Freedom

—Worth and dignity of the individual

—Equal opportunity

—Mutual responsibility

Our fundamental structures for preserving and enhancing these basic values are:

—Representative government: one person, one vote

—Separation of powers

—Freedom of religion, speech, and assembly

—Freedom of the press

—A system of justice grounded on due process and presumption of innocence

—Universal public education

Any investigation of the role of private philanthropy in the United States must attend to these basic values and social institutions.

1. Getting a Perspective on the Relative Importance of Private Philanthropy

Philanthropy serves to preserve these values and structures. As important as philanthropy is, it must be seen in the perspective of serving the basic values and fundamental institutions, not transcending them. Simultaneously, philanthropy provides for individual expression, creativity, alternatives and options, criticism, reform, and even outrage. (Senator Daniel Patrick Moynihan suggests that it may not be too far-fetched to ascribe the longevity of our democracy to the availability of outlets for outrage.)

There is always a tendency to reach back into history to come up with our examples of the impact of philanthropy, and the record is glorious: abolition of slavery, creation of pubic schools and public libraries, women's suffrage, child labor laws, and the like. But this suggests that those halcyon days are long past.

President Reagan has provided welcome attention to the voluntary side of the United States but, along the way, he has contributed to the view that in earlier times Americans were far more willing than we are today to help one another and to become involved in causes and public issues. It is almost a given that we are now a less caring society and that we should worry about what has happened to all that neighborliness, public-spiritedness, and charity.

Actually, the past was not as good as it is remembered, and the present is better than it is perceived. A far larger proportion and many more parts of our population are involved in community activity today than at any time in our history. We organize to influence every conceivable aspect of the human condition and are willing to stand up and be counted on almost any public issue. We organize to fight zoning changes, approve bond issues, oppose or propose abortion, improve garbage collection, expose overpricing, enforce equal rights, or protest wars.

As contrasted to those "good old days," in very recent times we have successfully organized to deal with a vast array of human needs and aspirations. These include the rights of women, conservation and preservation, learning disabilities, conflict resolution, Hispanic culture and rights, education on the free enterprise system, the aged, voter registration, the environment, Native Americans, the dying, experimental theater, international understanding, drunk driving, population control, neighborhood empowerment, control of nuclear power, and consumerism.

A 1981 Gallup survey commissioned by Independent Sector indicates that 47 percent of adults are volunteers. Thirty-one percent give at least two hours each week, and one out of every ten devotes at least seven hours every week to volunteer assignments. The dollar value of all this contributed time is conservatively estimated at $65 billion.

The base of participation is also spreading. There are more young people, more men, and more older people. Every economic group is involved. There are more people who have problems themselves. The mutual help movement is the fastest growing side of the voluntary sector. For almost every problem, there is now a group of people who have weathered the storm and are reaching out to help others newly faced with depression, divorce, abuse, or heart surgery.

To the surprise of all who have matter-of-factly assumed that with so many women now in the work force, it is harder to find female volunteers, the happy reality is that there are more women serving as volunteers now than in the past. Indeed, the Gallup survey reveals the fascinating information that the woman who works is more likely to volunteer than the woman who does not.

Incidentally, but hardly incidental, it has been interesting and revealing to realize that when one thinks of the giants of this sector, one is likely to think of women, including Clara Barton, Jane Addams, Mary McLeod Bethune, Susan B. Anthony, Dorothea Dix, Alice Paul, Elizabeth Cady Stanton, Harriet Beecher Stowe, Dorothy Day, Mother Seton, Carrie Nation, Margaret Sanger, Lucretia Mott, and Harriet Tubman. It is the only one of the three sectors that really taps the full spectrum of the nation's talent.

One of the reasons so little is known and so many misconceptions exist about volunteering and philanthropy generally is that this is an aspect of our national life that we take for granted and have never really felt a need to study. Now that there seems to be a growing realization that community service is a vital part of our national character, there is greater interest in having a clearer grasp of the facts, trends, and impact.

Misunderstanding exists on the financial side also. Most people assume that foundations and corporations represent a very large proportion of giving in America. As important as their dollars are, the two combined represent only 10 percent of all that is given. Ninety percent comes from individuals.

Most people assume that wealthy individuals represent the bulk of personal giving but, in fact, just about half of all charitable dollars come from families with incomes under $25,000. Also, people with incomes of $5,000 to $10,000 contribute two and one-half times more of their income than do people with incomes of $50,000 to $100,000 (3.9 percent compared to 1.6 percent). Even in families with incomes of $5,000 or less, the average given in 1981 was $238, about 5 percent of their income.

A Gallup survey on giving illustrates that in 1981, 86 percent of all American adults made contributions to the causes of their choice. We gave $60 billion, an average of more than $500 per person. We are the only nation in the world where giving and volunteering are pervasive characteristics of the total population.

2. The Specific Role of the Voluntary, Philanthropic Sector

The litany of specific roles begins quite naturally with our decisions as a people as to what constitutes the public business. It has been through our voluntary associations that public responsibility has been defined. As others have pointed out so often, many of the services now understood to be public responsibility began with voluntary institutions: education, care of orphans, shelter for the destitute elderly, and the like. All of the great social movements had their origins in this nonprofit sector: abolition, women's suffrage, child labor laws, and so forth. These advocacy, experimentation, and reform efforts were central in deciding public responsibility.

The advocacy role also relates to the needs of groups of individuals. For many voluntary organizations, advocacy is their best service. Advocacy is often a greater contribution to advancing the needs and rights of autistic children than running one facility for them. It also involves our ideas for better zoning laws, improved foreign policy, or protection of the ozone layer.

Voluntary organizations have always represented our options and alternatives for doing things in our own way or for trying to demonstrate that there is a better way. Throughout our society, there are parallel systems of public and private schools, colleges, libraries, museums, research institutes, recreation facilities, day-care centers, and the like. They are a reflection of our diversity, search for excellence, and freedom to experiment.

Beyond the urgent causes and crusades, the independent sector simply provides people a chance to do their own thing, i.e., to be different, to be a bit freer, to be unique. In *The Endangered Sector*, Waldemar Nielsen summarizes the variety of interests that Americans freely pursue through their voluntary organizations:

"If your interest is people, you can help the elderly by a contribution to the Grey Panthers; or teenagers, through the Jean Teen Scene of Chicago; or young children through your local nursery school; or everyone by giving to the Rock of All Ages in Philadelphia.

"If your interest is animals, there is the ASCPA and Adopt-A-Pet; if fishes, the Izaak Walton League; if birds, the American Homing Pigeon Institute or the Easter Bird Banding Association.

"If you are a WASP, there is the English Speaking Union and the Mayflower Descendants Association; if you have a still older association with the country, there is the Redcliff Chippewa Fund or the Museum of the American Indian.

"If your vision is local, there is the Cook County Special Bail Project and Clean Up the Ghetto in Philadelphia; if national, there is America the Beautiful; if global, there is the United Nations Association; if celestial there are the Sidewalk Astronomers of San Francisco.

If you are interested in tradition and social continuity, there is the society for the Preservation of Historic Landmarks and the Portland Friends of Cast Iron Architecture; if social change is your passion, there is Common Cause; and if that seems too sober for you, there is the Union of Radical Political Economists or perhaps the Theatre for Revolutionary Satire in New York.

"If your pleasure is music, there is a supermarket of choices—from Vocal Jazz to the Philharmonic Society to the American Guild of English Hand Bellringers.

"If your don't know quite what you want, there is Get Your Head Together, Inc. of Glen Ridge, New Jersey. If your interests are contradictory, there is the Great Silence Broadcasting Foundation of California. If they are ambiguous, there is the Tombstone Health Service of Arizona."[1]

Though Nielsen's delightful enumeration mentions creativity, that contribution of philanthropy and voluntary action deserves special mention. Whether it is dance, opera, or other areas of human creativity, this sector provides the opportunity and the freedom to try something new. It might be an absolutely new way of treating drug dependency, a new exchange of people from different cultures, or starting a foundation to try to identify and fund geniuses. John Gardner says, "Perhaps the most striking feature of the sector is its relative freedom from constraints and its resulting pluralism. Within the bounds of the law, all kinds of people can pursue any idea or program they wish. Unlike government, any independent sector group need not ascertain that its idea or philosophy is supported by some large constituency, and unlike the business sector, they do not need to pursue only those ideas which will be profitable. If a handful of people want to back a new idea, they need seek no larger consensus."[2]

One of the largest roles of voluntary organizations is religious expression and protection of that freedom. As incredible as it might seem, we tend to get so preoccupied with direct human services that we usually leave out the churches from our discussion of voluntary organizations. But working on *America's Voluntary Spirit*, I was wrenched back to an awareness of how much of the tradition *and* services *and* advocacy of this sector relate to the earliest determinations of freedom of religion. We have tended to set aside that whole one-half of our sector as though it did not really belong, i.e., that portion relating largely to salvation, but if you look at what the conscience, the meeting ground, and the organized neighborliness represented by the churches have meant to the kind of society we are, organized religion takes on a different and larger significance. And we do not have to go back in history for examples. Who has been more in the forefront of the public business of the homeless and the resettlement of refugees? And who has provided a forum for such different messengers as Jesse Jackson and Jerry Falwell—so different that people on the one side want to narrow the definition of religion to protect us from the other side? In a recent *Christian Science Monitor* article I said, "Don't save me from the left or the right."[3]

3. Can We Depend on Philanthropy to Continue to Fulfill These Functions?

As indicated above, there are many roles and values that philanthropic institutions represent, including providing services and acting as vehicles through which the government fulfills some of its public responsibilities, but the largest contribution is the independence they provide for innovation, excellence, criticism, and, where necessary, reform.

None of this is to suggest that nonprofit activity is more important or can take the place of democratic government. We lose our perspective on the sector and society when we exaggerate the importance of private philanthropy and voluntary organizations, particularly when we put them ahead of our responsibility to democratic government. More attention by the schools and the public at large would help people sort out and understand how this country does its public business. In some quarters, there is an exaggerated interpretation of what voluntary organizations should and can do and what government should not do. Some see voluntary effort as getting in the way of governmental responsibility. Others preach that voluntary organizations should do it all. Obviously, we need both strong government and a strong voluntary sector, but we will have neither if the public does not understand the relative roles and its responsibility to each.

The crucial consequence for philanthropy and society of confusing the relative roles of the voluntary and public sectors is a reduced emphasis on the independence of voluntary organizations. Between the efforts of voluntary organizations to attract government dollars and government's growing efforts to regulate nonprofit activity, the quintessential contribution and quality of independence is being dimmed.

In that *Christian Science Monitor* article I say, "Liberals who for 50 years have been listening to their Roman Catholic priests tell them how to vote, or who still hear their Black preachers endorse candidates, or who encouraged their Lutheran ministers to march in Selma, want to clamp down on what can be done in the name of religion. Conservatives, who preach faith in people, minimal government, and clearer separation of church and state, want expansion of governmental control over what they define as unholy.

"If both sides get their way, we'll have more laws to protect us from the right and the left—and less freedom for everyone.

"Out of passion and bitterness, both sides are losing sight of protection of the larger freedoms of religion, speech and assembly, and their wide-open opportunities to spread what they consider the truth. Any infringement on these freedoms and opportunities will sooner or later infringe both of them and all of us."[4]

My greatest concern by far about the future of the voluntary sector is the gradual loss of the independence of the organizations within it. As more and more voluntary organizations become dependent on government funds, these organizations lose a very real part of their independence, and as government becomes more and more the funder of so-called independent organizations, government assumes that it has a greater right to oversee their voluntary partners *and* the whole of the voluntary sector.

Let me be specific about some of the problems that amount to the loss of independence.

A. Problems in Relationships with Government which Result in an Erosion of Independence of Private Philanthropy

(1) Dependence on Government Funding and Related Governmental Controls over Voluntary Institutions. This country has always relied on public/private partnerships to carry out public services. In all areas of public responsibility—education, health, social services, and the like—nonprofit organizations assist in the delivery of public services and are compensated for it. In the past twenty-five years, this source of income grew far faster than the other two principal sources of income: contributions and fees for service. For the sector as a whole, it represents the highest proportion of income. This involves grants in aid, formula grants, categorical grants, block grants, project grants, fees for service, interest subsidies, vouchers, loan guarantees, credit insurance, purchase agreements, surplus land grants, and many other forms of governmental assistance. The number and complexity of such arrangements and the total and proportion of monies involved require necessary accountability mechanisms, but in many cases impose undue control on the voluntary operation. Under the best of circumstances, dependence on government funding diminishes some degree of independence, and in the worst circumstances it destroys independence altogether.

(2) Challenges to Tax Deductions. By far, the largest of Independent Sector's current activities involves efforts to convince the Administration and Congress not to remove tax incentives for contributions. Current Treasury proposals, if enacted, would reduce giving by 21 percent.

(3) The Consequences when Contributions are Considered a "Tax Expenditure." For very good reasons, the government keeps track of how much money is lost to the federal Treasury when people deduct mortgage payments, health care costs, or contributions. The problem is that a number of people within government are beginning to say something like, "If these are monies that the government has forgone, shouldn't government have more to say about how these contributions are channeled and spent?" This brings prejudice into the arena where it least belongs.

(4) Confusion and Debate about Relative Roles of Governmental and Voluntary Institutions. Federal, state, and local officials are making a fuller assessment of the relative roles of public and private institutions. This increasingly involves all three sectors, for example, in the current confusion and competition among government, nonprofit, and profit-making hospitals.

In 1984, the Small Business Administration issued a report called "Unfair Competition by Nonprofit Organizations with Small Business—An Issue for the 1980s." In essence, it says that nonprofit organizations are using their tax exempt advantage to compete unfairly with their profit-making counterparts and that, in keeping with our commitment to free enterprise, where a service can be provided by a profit-making organization, it should have the job.

(5) Challenges to Earned Income. The IRS and many federal courts have increasingly challenged the "unrelated business income" of nonprofit organizations. This comes at the very time when corporation and foundation contributors and citizen boards are calling on voluntary organizations

to be more entrepreneurial. The Government Accounting Office (GAO) has recently been given the go-ahead by the Congressional Joint Committee on Taxation to do a major new study of the "unrelated" income of nonprofit organizations with emphasis on testing labs, university research, and child care.

(6) Challenges to Advocacy Efforts. The Action agency's efforts to close down VISTA (Volunteers in Service to America) and other activist efforts, OMB's several challenges to the advocacy rights and activities of voluntary organizations, and the Office of Personnel Management's determined exclusion of advocacy organizations from the Combined Federal Campaign are examples of the government's discomfort with advocacy, particularly when it represents a vehicle for criticism of public activity. The attitude that voluntary *service* is to be applauded and *advocacy* curtailed ignores the reality that most of the best voluntary efforts in our history are related to those efforts which advocated most of the public programs we take pride in today.

Most of the great movements of our society have had their origins in this independent sector. Some who led those efforts were viewed as unpopular, troublesome, rabble-rousing, and maybe even dangerous. One of our largest responsibilities is to keep open the freedoms that will allow their successors to establish the new causes of tomorrow. There is no greater danger to our liberty than allowing those in power to have any great control over their potential reformers.

(7) State Laws and Local Ordinances Governing Public Participation. In the name of orderliness and protection of the people, a growing number of states and communities are narrowly defining who can petition, march, raise funds, or do other things to attract public attention and support for public causes. Twice in the period from 1982 to 1985, Independent Sector successfully challenged state laws and local ordinances which would have severely limited the free speech and assembly rights of voluntary organizations.

(8) Changes in the Definition of Public Charities and What They Can Do. There are regular efforts through regulation or legislation to more narrowly define what is a public charty [501(C) (3)] organization and what these organizations can do. For instance, in 1983 we successfully challenged an internal IRS ruling that would have resulted in major restrictions on the voter education rights of nonprofit groups.

(9) Challenges to the Property Tax Exemption. An increasing number of communities, strapped for funds for essential services, are challenging the property tax exemption of many nonprofit organizations and imposing user fees. In Washington, DC, for instance, a decision, fortunately beaten back, would have restricted a church's property tax exemption to the proportion of the organization's time devoted strictly to worship. The organization's social services would not have counted.

(10) The List Goes On. These are just examples of challenges to the independence of nonprofit organizations. Each is serious in itself, but together they represent a frightening threat to the future capacity of such organizations to freely represent the organized influence of citizens.

Though it may sound self-serving, I am absolutely comfortable that had not Independent Sector been formed in 1980, states and counties would have continued in their trend towards tighter restriction on philanthropy; the IRS would have limited greatly the voter education rights of voluntary organizations; the Office of Management and Budget would have succeeded in its end run around the freedom of voluntary organizations to represent their clients and causes; the Small Business Administration and GAO would have succeeded in their challenge to the entrepreneurial and earned income rights of nonprofit organizations; and the Treasury would have further undercut the encouragement of charitable contributions. Our largest single purpose is to protect the independence of voluntary organizations to be the free agents of free people.

B. *Impact of Federal Cutbacks*

I will take no time to repeat many of the consequences of federal budget cuts for essential public services performed by voluntary institutions, but it is important to call attention to the utter contradiction between reducing support of such organizations by both direct budget cuts and removal of some of the tax incentives, while at the same time calling upon voluntary organizations to expand their services to people.

C. *Relative Declines in Giving*

For most of the last 15 years, though the totals of contributions have risen, the proportion they represent of Personal Income and of Gross National Product declined, even at a time when the disposable income of the significant majority of Americans has risen dramatically. Also, the average contributions of wealthy individuals have been declining steadily. Since 1981, the giving by persons with incomes between $200,000 and $500,000 has dropped 17 percent, and for persons with incomes over $1 million it has dropped 3.9 percent. Imagine what that does to those crucial leadership gifts and to the establishment and growth of foundations.

D. *Indications of Less Commitment by Educated Young People Toward Community Service*

A recent study by Yankelovich, Skelly, and White for the Rockefeller Brothers Fund has found that younger persons between the ages of eighteen and thirty-four do not place community service high among their values. Conversely, the study finds that the primary motivations for community service and giving relate to religious conviction and commitment to country, neither of which is generally strong with people under thirty-five.

Though it is less objective, my own experience supports these findings. In regular meetings with younger people, I find an alarming lack of awareness of the importance of voluntary participation, giving, and associations. Young people are almost cynical about giving and volunteering, and especially about philanthropic and voluntary organizations; yet these are the same people who appropriately remind us how important it is to "do your own thing" or "have control of your own destiny" or "be empowered." They do not seem to grasp that it is often through our voluntary organizations that these opportunities are realized.

E. *Lack of Public Awareness of the Role and Importance of Citizen Participation*

Independent Sector's Organizing Committee says, "One of the problems faced by the sector is that it is both everywhere and invisible. We are all involved with many of its organizations but don't recognize its roles and even its existence as a distinctive sector. People take for granted the freedoms it provides and sustains. We are not really aware of what a precious aspect of our freedom is embodied in it."

F. *Awareness of and Training for Active Citizenship and Personal Community Service are Rarely Part of Academic Efforts to Help Develop "The Educated Person"*

Alan Pifer, former President of the Carnegie Corporation, went through more than fifty textbooks used in civics, history, social studies, and the like, and found no reference to philanthropy and voluntary organizations. He points out that one can go through a full and supposedly thorough formal education without ever hearing or reading about the major role of the voluntary sector in American life.

If the problems and trends persist, and if responsible leaders and institutions do not accentuate the essential role of active citizenship and voluntary action, this central factor of our freedom will no longer be sufficient to the task. In his seminal work, "Major Challenges to Philanthropy," Robert Payton, President of the Exxon Education Foundation, ends with this frightening thought: "...[T]he new Britanica overlooks philanthropy, as far as I can tell, although its predecessors dealt with it quite adequately. That's the way it goes: one day you take it for granted, and the next day it's gone."[5]

4. Conclusion

Beyond the figures, activities, and causes served, participation and pluralism have had great influence on the kind of people we are. In "American Philanthropy and the National Character," historian Merle Curti states, "Emphasis on voluntary initiative...has helped give America her national character...All these philanthropic initiatives give support to the thesis that philanthropy has helped to shape national character...[by] implementing the idea that America is a process rather than a finished product."[6]

More than two hundred fifty years ago, Cotton Mather, in *Bonifacius: An Essay To Do Good*, preached that doing good was "sound policy, an honor, a privilege, an incomparable pleasure, and a reward in itself." He also said, "Pious example, moral leadership, voluntary effort, and private charity were the means by which competing and conflicting interests in society might be brought into harmony."[7]

In the chapter "Raising Money," in *Up From Slavery*, Booker T. Washington concludes, "While the work of going from door to door and from office to office is hard, disagreeable, and costly in bodily strength, yet it has some compensations. Such work gives one a rare opportunity to study human nature. It also has its compensations in giving one an opportunity to meet some of the best people in the world—to be more correct, I think I should say *the best* people in the world. When one takes a broad survey of the country, he will find that the most useful and influential people in it are those who take the deepest interest in institutions that exist for the purpose of making the world better."[8]

What comes through from all of the great citizen movements of our history is that the participation, the caring, and the evidence that people can make a difference add wonderfully to the spirit of our society. Inez Haynes Irwin, in *The Story of Alice Paul*, repeatedly refers to the *spirit* of those women, not only in deciding on the task and accomplishing it, but in what their success meant to them as human beings. "They developed a sense of devotion to their ideal of freedom which would have stopped short of no personal sacrifice, not death itself. They developed a sense of comradeship for each other which was half love, half admiration and all reverence. In summing up a fellow worker, they speak first of her spirit, and her spirit is always *beautiful*, or *noble* or *glorious*."[9]

It is clear that when people make the effort, not only are causes and other people helped, but something very special happens to the giver too and, in the combination, the community and the nation take on a spirit of compassion, comradship, and confidence. Although it is important not to exaggerate the worth of philanthropy, it is also important not to underestimate how much this participation means to our freedom as individuals and as a society. Its opportunity to continue to do so will be in direct relation to its future degree of independence.

NOTES

[1]Waldemar Nielsen, *The Endangered Sector* (New York: Columbia University Press, 1979).

[2]John Gardner, Address to Charter Meeting of Independent Sector, March 5, 1980.

[3]Brian O'Connell, "Don't save me from the left or right," *Christian Science Monitor*, December 28, 1983, p. 12.

[4]*ibid.*

[5]Robert Payton, "Major Challenges to Philanthropy," paper presented to Independent Sector, September 1984.

[6]Merle Curti, "American Philanthropy and the National Character."

[7]Cotton Mather, *Bonifacius: An Essay Upon the Good*, ed. David Levin (Gainesville, FL: Scholars Facsimilies and Reprints, 1967).

[8]Booker T. Washington, *Up From Slavery* (New York: Dell Publishing Co., Inc. 1965), p. 132.

[9]Inez Haynes Irwin, *The Story of Alice Paul: And the National Women's Party* (Fairfax, VA: Denlingers Publishers, Ltd., 1964).

PRIVATE PHILANTHROPY AND PUBLIC POLICY: A HISTORICAL APPRAISAL

Peter Dobkin Hall

How Americans Make Public Policy

> But the law of inheritance was the last step to equality. I am surprised that ancient and modern jurists have not attributed to this law a greater influence on human affairs. It is true that these laws belong to civil affairs; but they ought, nevertheless, to be placed at the head of all political institutions; for they exercise an incredible influence upon the social state of a people, while political laws show only what this state already is. They have, moreover, a sure and uniform manner of operating upon society, affecting, as it were, generations yet unborn. Through their means man acquires a kind of preternatural power over the future lot of his fellow creatures.
>
> —Alexis de Tocqueville[1]

Tocqueville's assessment of the effect of the laws of inheritance on society applies equally well to our peculiar system of private philanthropy and its influence on the making of public policy. In theory, public policy in a democratic society emerges from the deliberations of public bodies, legislative and judicial. But, as Tocqueville suggests, these show the state only as it "already is," representing only the final and most visible—and, very often, least significant—stages of the policy process. To be sure, the words and deeds of political actors and the activities of the institutions they comprise are important and worthy of attention in themselves. But they do not begin to explain the most important aspects of the policy process: (1) the mechanisms through which areas of activity in society come to be defined as public policy problems; (2) the mechanisms which shape

---

*The research from which this paper is drawn has been funded by grants from the Exxon Education Foundation, the Teagle Foundation, the American Council of Learned Societies, and the Program on Non-Profit Organizations, Yale University.

the perception of problems amenable to public policy (and thereby implicitly suggest solutions to these problems); and (3) the interpersonal and institutional alliance systems which not only comprise these definitional and perceptual mechanisms, but which also permit politicians and jurists to make the decisions which embody the tenets of public policy.

As Tocqueville described them, our laws of inheritance, which favored the division of property, promoted individualism and an overall social and economic equality. Similarly, our tendency until this century to allocate fundamental tasks of education, health care, social welfare, religion, and culture to bodies other than the state transformed the policy process. Rather than being a fairly straightforward matter of formal actions by political institutions and their operatives, it became a highly complex one involving formal and informal voluntary associations which, while sometimes acting to implement the intentions of the state, more often endeavored to influence those intentions either by acting as bases of organized support for politicians favoring their causes or, more frequently, by attempting to set the moral and perceptual agendas which serve as the bases for political action.

It is true that political parties are private voluntary associations. But their peculiarly close relation to the state and their essentially coalitional character render them particularly unsuitable as arenas for the delineation of moral and perceptual agendas. As with the state itself, the ideological and epistemological premises underlying formal legislative and judicial action must be broadly held—and hence implicit—before statutes are written and decisions made. Attempts to deal with issues of this kind in legislative forums lead inevitably (as in the nineteenth-century debates over slavery or in contemporary ones over abortion) to deadlock or, at worst, violent conflict. For this reason, the fundamental tasks of moral and perceptual consensus building have tended to lie outside of explicitly political and governmental bodies.

Ironically, the same mechanisms that restrict the moral and perceptual agenda-setting capacities of political bodies also limit the political power of religious organizations. Just as a political party's effectiveness is based on its ability to forge coalitions between the largest possible number of voters—which, from a practical standpoint, requires it to pass over fundamental issues of morality—so the ecclesiastical body, if it wishes to bring in the maximum number of communicants, must avoid those secular issues which might drive away potential members or divide the organization. Of course, a church is free to be political—just as political parties are free to concern themselves with morality. But they do so at their peril. Historically, such narrowly based entities are either short-lived or extremely limited in their impact: moralistic political parties (the Prohibitionists, for example) and political religions (such as the communitarian pietist sects) have not been notably successful in America.

Voluntary Associations and the Problem of Moral Authority

Political parties and churches aside, the universe of voluntary associations is very large. As Tocqueville noted:

> Americans of all ages, all conditions, and all dispositions constantly form associations. They have not only commercial and manufacturing companies, in which all take part, but associations of a thousand other kinds, religious, moral, serious, futile, general or restricted, enormous or diminutive. The Americans make associations to give entertainments, to found seminaries, to build inns, to construct churches, to diffuse books, to send missionaries to the antipodes; in this manner they found hospitals, prisons, and schools. Wherever at the head of some new undertaking you see the government in France, or a man of rank in England, in the United States you will be sure to find an association.[2]

But the ubiquity of the association and its accessibility to every element in the population in no way suggest that all associations are equally significant. Most are directed to the accomplishment of limited objectives involving finite groups in particular localities. Some, however, have more universal and public purposes: education, care of the poor and dependent, public health, the pursuit of science, the exercise of religion. These associations are characterized by open-ended purposes, are devoted to general classes of persons, and define and pursue moral and perceptual agendas.

Although organized by private citizens, the impact of associations is public. While subject in theory to the same market pressures affecting political parties and churches, they are in practice less so because the utility of the goods and services they provide—education, health care, culture, and so on—is not a function of quantity but of quality: the measure of educational achievement is not how many students pass through the classroom, but the success with which certain things are learned; the measure of medical achievement is not how many patients receive attention, but the degree of success with which their illnesses and injuries are cured; and the measure of aesthetic achievement is not the number of persons who see or read a work of art, but the extent to which they are moved or persuaded by it.

If these private voluntary associations differ from others in their essentially technical and qualitative character, they are also set apart by certain unusual fiscal and structural features. While the receipt of fees for the goods and services they provide has always been an important part of their income, historically they have also received substantial revenues—usually in the form of donations and bequests—which were not payments for services. Their purpose has been to enhance the effectiveness of the recipient organization, either by reducing the cost or enlarging the scope of the services it offers. Revenues of this kind have an additional unusual feature: because of the "charitable" purposes to which they are devoted and because of the open-endedness of the class of persons which will be benefited by

them, the law permits donors and recipient organizations to set them up
as perpetual trusts to be devoted forever to the accomplishment of certain
designated purposes. Finally, these associations are distinguished from the
broad category of voluntary associations by the fact that they do not earn
or distribute profits among their directors or employees. Organizations
sharing these features are, in America, the chief beneficiaries of
philanthropy.

But what do philanthropy and this peculiar class of moral and perceptual agenda-setting private voluntary organizations have to do with the
public policy process? Tocqueville, in writing of political associations,
noted:

> In America the citizens who form the minority associate in order, first,
> to show their numerical strength and so to diminish the moral power
> of the majority; and, secondly, to stimulate competition and thus
> discover those arguments that are most fitted to act upon the majori-
> ty; for they always entertain hopes of drawing over the majority to
> their own side, and then controlling the supreme power in its name.[3]

Although nonpolitical private voluntary associations seldom concern
themselves with explicitly electoral goals, they are nonetheless concerned
with assertions of moral power, the discovery of arguments most fitted
to act upon the majority, and hopes of drawing over the majority to their
own side. They differ from political bodies, however, in that their activities
focus not on influencing how people vote, but on how they think, feel,
and perceive the issues and personalities on which they vote. They are, in
sum, the sources of moral authority that govern the direction of public life.

Voluntary Associations, Philanthropy, and Public Policy: the Historical Problem

The peculiar character of private voluntary associations in America is
not derived from their intrinsic organizational characteristics, but from
the set of historical circumstances in which they developed and the ideology
and social characteristics of the groups most active and effective in promoting their development. Private voluntary associations do not date from
the earliest years of settlement. Although the early colonial churches and
townships in many ways resembled—and provided organizational models
for—associations, and although they shared a common conception of
sovereignty (in which authority was seen to flow from the people to
organizations, whether congregants or electors, rather than from organizations to the populace), the private voluntary association only began to appear with any frequency in the second half of the eighteenth century.

The circumstances under which voluntary associations arose merit particular attention, for they determined the allocation of fundamental moral
and perceptual agenda-setting functions outside the realms of religion and
politics. Until the 1750s, virtually all the basic activities of economic,

social, political, and cultural life were mediated through the family. Because most Americans were subsistence farmers, the family was the basic unit of both production and consumption. Even those few hundred families of merchants, professionals, and artisans who did subsist from market relationships, "reaping where they did not sow and gathering where they did not winnow," operated firms in which family organization was largely identical with the organization of production.[4] Aspirants to the crafts, professions, and commerce were trained through apprenticeship, in which they entered the household of an established practitioner and were subject to his authority both as father and master.[5] And the duties of the master included not only the passing on of technical competence, but also instruction in the fundamentals of morality and literacy.[6] Members of the household were the source of most labor; the kinship network both supplied capital and defined the range of occupational opportunities open to individuals.[7] The family also cared for the poor and dependent, both by caring for their own and by being entrusted with the care of others by the civil authorities.[8]

Political life until the Revolutionary Era—and in some places for some decades afterwards—was similarly mediated by the family. While in theory any male over twenty-one possessed of a certain amount of property could vote, the ability to own property was generally determined by parental decisions to grant it.[9] Electoral success almost invariably depended on kinship and, if the goal was high office, on alliances between major family groups.[10] The importance of family on both local and state levels is abundantly illustrated by the remarkable persistence of certain officeholding families for generations.

Even in culture—the ministry and education—the family was the key element. While pulpits could not be passed on from father to son like other forms of property, clerical dynasties tended to be the rule in New England rather than the exception.[11] And to the extent that formal education was dominated by the ministry (the minister serving either as schoolmaster or as the dominant figure in the "society" which governed the schools), education on all levels felt the force of family power.

The rise of voluntary organizations in America coincided with the disintegration of this family-based system of organization. The primary reason for its collapse was, as Tocqueville suggested and modern social historians have confirmed, the system of partible inheritance.[12] The ideology and practice of family government required that parents possess the resources to concretely reward obedience to paternal authority. High birthrates and low mortality rapidly depleted common lands and diminished the size of shares in parental estates.[13] Strategies designed to consolidate and conserve these resources and thus maintain the system of family government proved to be self-defeating. Occupational and geographical mobility, two fundamental strategies designed to conserve family holdings, worked against the ability to maintain intergenerational authority and, because both required cash outlays, forced subsistence farmers into the impersonal market system. Parental attempts to defer granting land and permission to marry sparked intergenerational conflicts. Finally, as the resources of families eroded, they became less able to provide the public services of education, career-training, and care of the poor and dependent, which had traditionally been entrusted to them.

This crisis of the family as the central institution of colonial society underlay the more visible mid-eighteenth-century crises of religious and political life. The central feature of these crises involved the delegitimation of established institutions.[14] In religion, this delegitimation occurred less because of the challenge of such modern ideological forces as the Enlightenment than because of internal institutional conflict. One element of this conflict involved the increasingly diverse character of life in colonial America: the rise of the market system and of the urban concentrations associated with it produced social groups with distinctively different life styles and outlooks. The urban life style encouraged secularism and rationalism not only because of its intrinsic utility, but also because of the prestige and concrete advantages associated with cosmopolitan Enlightenment styles of thought and taste. Secular rationalism encouraged a works-oriented religious doctrine that was anathema to the more traditional Calvinists of the countryside. The divergence of urban and rural religious styles brought with it conflicts over doctrine and ecclesiastical authority whose ultimate effect was not only the fragmentation of denominational unity, but also the devaluation of the authority of established churches. While religion remained an important force in the lives of all Americans, denomination and doctrine became a matter of individual preference.

The most serious source of the delegitimation of religion was the family crisis itself. The distribution of common lands within large townships had led to the formation of new settlements within their boundaries. As these new settlements, or "outliver communities," became more established, their inhabitants began to petition for the establishment of their own churches, schools, and, in some cases, civic bodies. The older core settlements and churches in the towns generally opposed these efforts not only because such grants of autonomy would be costly in terms of losses of communicants and tax revenues, but also because they often represented efforts by younger members of family groups to reduce the extent of political and religious authority held by the older generation.

The bitterness of these disputes served primarily to factionalize towns and congregations, inevitably delegitimating effects. Churches came to be seen less as gatherings of believers than as political organizations, vehicles for factions struggling for the control of the community. By the 1730s, Protestantism in the colonies began to fragment as clusters of believers began to seek religious authenticity. This search led both to a major evangelical upthrust—the Great Awakening—and to the founding of a variety of radical alternatives to the established churches. While religion remained important for Americans, by the mid-eighteenth century it had begun to lose its public authority.

Government bodies underwent a similar delegitimation during the first half of the eighteenth century. First, the intergenerational conflicts stemming from the crisis of family resources undermined the system of deference on which traditional institutions like the town meeting had always depended. As patriarchal authority within the family declined, so did the overall structure of deference within communities. Indeed, as historians John Waters and Winthrop Jordan have pointed out, the paternal metaphor of political authority was turned on its head by Revolutionary generation, which justified its rebellion in terms of the righteousness of children standing against "unnatural fathers" who demanded obedience but lacked the resources to reward it.[15] Deprived of scriptural sanction and ethical force, government came increasingly to be seen as a mere vehicle for ambition. A second component of the delegitimation of the state involved a set of changes imposed from outside the colonies. Beginning with the Restoration of the Stuart monarchy in 1660, the British government had been struggling to bring the colonies under more direct control. Politically, this involved the annulment of the colonial charters and the replacement of elected governors by royal appointees. As struggles between the major European powers for control of North America intensified in the 1740s, and as English administrators became more directly involved in colonial economic and political life, colonial governments, in spite of the fact that they continued to elect their own legislatures, came increasingly to be seen as instruments both of an alien power and of self-aggrandizing merchant cliques. Finally, the ecclesiastical conflict stemming from the Great Awakening divided politicians into major factions which anticipated the formation of party organizations. This served to limit the moral authority not only of political operatives, but of the state itself.

In this context, both the American Revolution and the creation of a new form of government under the Constitution of 1787 can be seen as a search for authenticity and authority. The minimalization of government, embodied both in the post-Independence state constitutions and in the federal Constitution, eloquently expresses the profound suspicion Americans shared of government of any kind: it was at best viewed as a necessary evil. While religious establishments in some states would remain for decades after the enactment of the federal Bill of Rights, religion was clearly displaced from the position it had formerly occupied as the delimiter of public and private morality. (Even in places like Connecticut, the "Land of Steady Habits" where the Congregational church remained established until 1818, it was the subject of unremitting political attack and, as a result, declined both in numbers and in moral authority). The institutional crisis of the eighteenth century served to deprive government of the ethical sanction of tradition and scripture. It was this fact that freed the Founding Fathers of the constraints of past practice and denomination, enabling them to construct their new edifice on Reason and Common Sense. But this freedom was in itself constraining, for it required that major areas of power—those most relevant to the policy process, including power over public opinion and public morality—stand outside the realm of state control.

There is reason to believe that many of the founders of the New Republic believed that "all men are intellectuals": every man could and would decide public questions for himself and vote his conscience.[16] They found out very soon, however, that "not all men have the function of intellectuals," as major components of the population, particularly those who had stood against the federal Constitution or who were aggrieved by the fiscal and foreign policies of the new government, began to establish an *organized* political opposition—the Democratic Republicans, the first of the modern American political parties. The rise of parties was vehemently denounced by the Federalist political establishment and the Democratic victory of 1800 was seen as nothing less than a revolution (which in a significant though nonviolent sense it was).[17] This institutionalization of faction, however, had the salutory effect of making explicit what was already implicit in the Constitution: the fact that power in a society of equals would have to be a product of *voluntary association*, the gathering of individuals in pursuit of particular ends. The "function of intellectuals" would be exercised not by individuals as such but by individuals in groups which—as political parties, congregations, professional and fraternal societies, manufacturing companies, and so on—would articulate the common interest of individuals and translate them into action. To the extent that these actions involved or affected the public, they became the delimiters of public policy: it was through their ability to persuade or otherwise influence legislatures that their private interests became policy.

Public Policy in the New Republic, 1800-1860

Not surprisingly, the groups most acutely aware of the consequences of democracy in America were those who lost the most by it. Those who had once commanded deference by virtue of office (ministers) or lineage (old colonial dynasties) or wealth (merchants) suddenly found that these counted for little in the scramble for fame, fortune, and political office that emerged with the new century. They were a politically impotent minority which could not realistically nourish any hope of regaining power. At the same time, they recognized that political disenfranchisement did not entirely deprive them of opportunities for influence: the abstention of constitutional government from moral and perceptual agenda-making, combined with the capacity to freely form voluntary associations, made it possible for minorities like themselves to devote themselves to the production of knowledge, the propagation of values, and the training of leadership.

Although the Second Great Awakening (c. 1790-1840) is generally conceived of as a religious phenomenon, it was equally if not more significant as a political one. Like Europe's Holy Alliance, through which the conservative monarchies of Europe combined to combat the contagion of French revolutionary ideas, American evangelicals and their allies in the laity recognized that a republic which left moral and perceptual issues to be decided in the marketplace was a republic at hazard. As Lyman Beecher wrote in his *Plea to the West*:

> If we do fail in our great experiment of self-government, our destruction will be as signal as the birthright abandoned, the mercies abused, and the provocation offered to beneficent Heaven....No spasms are like the spasms of expiring liberty, no wailings such as her convulsions extort. It took Rome three hundred years to die; and our death, if we perish, will be as much more terrific as our intelligence and free institutions have given us more bone, and sinew, and vitality. May God hide me from the day when the dying agonies of my country shall begin![18]

The alternative to the potential disaster of *anomie*, which the evangelicals saw as the inevitable outcome of a politicized morality on the one hand and a marketplace morality on the other, involved a commitment to the creation of institutions whose purpose was the articulation of morality. At its base this "evangelical counteroffensive" was religious, involving the development of new forms of ecclesiastical outreach (including the Sunday school, the tract society, religious journalism, missionary activity, and evangelical services). No less important, however, were its semireligious and secular correlates: the establishment of schools, colleges, libraries, educational societies, lyceums, and reform organizations.[19] The organizational aggressiveness of the evangelicals, combined with the considerable financial resources of some of their supporters—the first large-scale American philanthropists—soon gave them virtual control of the emerging private sector of American culture.[20] The clarity with which they understood what they were doing is evident in the fierceness with which they defended their associations against political interference. As Daniel Webster argued in the 1819 Dartmouth College Case:

> The case before the court is not of ordinary importance, nor of everyday occurance. It affects not this college only, but every college, and all the literary institutions in the country. They have flourished, hitherto, and have become in a high degree respectable and useful to the community. They have all a common principle of existence—the inviolability of their charters. It will be dangerous, a most dangerous experiment, to hold these institutions subject to the rise and fall of popular parties, and the fluctuations of political opinions. If the franchise may at any time be taken away, or impaired, the property may also be taken away, or its use perverted. Benefactors will have no certainty of effecting the object of their bounty, and learned men will

be deterred from devoting themselves to the service of such institutions, from the precarious title of their officers. Colleges and halls
will be deserted by better spirits, and become a theater for the con-
tention of politics. Party and faction will be cherished in the places
consecrated to piety and learning. The consequences are neither remote
nor possible only. They are certain and immediate.[21]

Webster's argument for the autonomy of "literary institutions" from
government interference seems perfectly unexceptional from the standpoint
of today. But his political enemies knew well that he was speaking for what
amounted to a conspiracy. As one noted in 1821, putting words into the
mouths of the evangelicals in a pamphlet entitled *To the Public: Priestcraft
Exposed and Primitive Christianity Defined*, "when all the colleges are
under our control it will establish our sentiments and influence, so that
we can manage the civil government as we please."[22]

In state after state, battles were fought both in the courts and in the
legislatures over the degree of autonomy and wealth that voluntary association formed for charitable purposes should possess. In most of the Southern
states, where Jeffersonian anti-institutional and anticlerical influence was
strongest, private charities were disabled by the "Virginia Doctrine," which
expressed implacable hositility and fear towards private charities, the President of the state's Supreme Court arguing that "unless Virginia acted
quickly to curb bequests to religious organizations, the 'whole property
of society' would be 'swallowed up in the insatiable gulph of public
charities.' "[23] In such a climate of opinion, it is hardly surprising that the
South did not become a seedbed for private voluntary activity.

The South was not alone, however, in its apprehensions about the power
of private voluntary organizations. New York, in many ways, exemplifies
the ways in which the enemies of these bodies acted to frustrate their
growth. In the revision of the state's statutes produced by the Jacksonian
legislatures of the late 1820s, the amount of property that could be held
by voluntary organizations was regulated by the state, the activities of these
organizations were made subject to the oversight of the Regents of the
University of the State of New York, testators were limited in the proportion of estates that could be designated for charitable purposes, and bequests were forbidden to organizations which were not yet in existence or
which had not received legislative sanction for enlarging their holdings.[24]
The impact of these laws on the growth of voluntary organizations through
the late nineteenth century was dramatic: Columbia College remained small
and poor, for its student body was only one-fifth that of Yale or Harvard,
and its endowment comprised less than one-tenth the value of its neighbors
to the East.[25] Although rising rapidly as a financial and commercial center,
New York City would not become the center of the nation's cultural life
until the 1890s, when the legislature removed the state's restrictions on
charity.

The New England states, which were the headwaters of the evangelical stream, also proved to be the center of legal liberality towards voluntary organizations. By the 1830s, Connecticut had passed a uniform corporation statute which freed incorporators from the burden of political lobbying for charters. In the same decade, the Massachusetts courts handed down a set of decisions—most importantly *Harvard College v. Amory*, which set institutional trustees apart from legal constraints on the investment of endowment funds, and *Nightingale v. Burrell*, which incorporated the Rule Against Perpetuities into American law and in so doing clearly differentiated charitable and testamentary trusts.[26] Unrestrained by legal fetters, New England's charitable institutions grew and flourished. While philanthropic bequests and gifts became the norm in nearly every town in the region, they assumed particular importance with the rise of great industrial fortunes after 1820 and the willingness of those in possession of such fortunes to concentrate their philanthropy on a handful of Boston-based institutions. Although hundreds of private voluntary associations were founded in Massachusetts between 1800 and 1860, and a great proportion of them held endowments, the vast majority of the state's philanthropy flowed in a few great streams. In 1860, Samuel Atkins Eliot analyzed the philanthropy of Bostonians during the previous fifteen years: of the $5 million dollars given for religious, charitable, educational, and miscellaneous projects (famine relief, the erection of monuments, and so on), 40 percent went to five institutions, namely, Harvard College, the Boston Public Library, Massachusetts General Hospital, the Boston Atheneum, and the Association for the Relief of Aged and Indigent Females.[27] Moreover, as Ronald Story showed in his brilliant and lucid *Forging of an Aristocracy*, the large donations of a small number of wealthy individuals made up the most significant component of this outpouring of philanthropy.

The combination of private wealth with evangelical zeal gave New England's "literary institutions"—and those founded by migrant New Englanders as they spread across the newly settled West and South—a peculiar power to shape opinion. While the opponents of private action were free to establish government agencies to deal with education, public health, and social welfare, they seldom did—either because conflicts between constituencies within the legislatures were too acute to permit major public commitments to such controversial areas, or because the public simply did not believe that it was worth spending public money on such things. The result was that private agencies underwritten by private philanthropy became agenda-setting bodies for the public as much by default as by intention. The significance of this situation would not emerge, however, until the Civil War, when the extraordinary challenge of organizing a modern military force and mobilizing the industrial capacity of the North pointed out the failure of Jeffersonian and Jacksonian administrative practices. These tasks, as a succession of Union disasters made clear, required expertise, professionalism, and an understanding of the importance of hierarchical organizations. The ultimate victory of the Union was seen by many as a vindication of private cultural institutions and their supporters: for it had been in the private sector, profit and nonprofit, that expertise had been fostered and, the character and values necessary for national discipline had been shaped in the decades before the war.

But the real test of the private sector came after the Civil War, as the country faced the tasks of Reconstruction, national economic development, and accommodating itself to a new industrial and urban order. The war itself had set a precedent for government activism, exemplified in the Pacific Telegraph Act of 1860, which authorized the government to construct a telegraph line from Missouri to San Francisco, and in the Pacific Railroad Act of 1860, which authorized the government to underwrite the construction of a transcontinental railway. And as government expanded its tasks, public policy in the modern sense of the term came into being. Because these new initiatives demanded commitments that were both large-scale and long-term, public policy could no longer be a series of single, uncoordinated acts. Enabling legislation had to proceed from a rationale which integrated and systematized decisions. And the implementation of these decisions, if they were to have any promise of success, would have to be carried out by trained personnel—civil servants—not political appointees who came and went with changes in administration. Finally, from a practical political standpoint, binding policy decisions of this kind would have to proceed from a consensus, a set of shared values and perceptions that transcended party.

Public Health Policy in Massachusetts, 1720-1870: A Case Study

As it happened, there was already a set of precedents for both the formulation and implementation of public policy that had been developing in the states since the 1830s. With the growth of large urban concentrations and the consequent rise of epidemic disease and other manifestations of poverty, overcrowding, and lack of civic foresight, voluntary associations began to devote themselves to problems of public health and welfare. Barbara Guttman Rosenkrantz's 1972 study, *Public Health and the State*, gave a particularly lucid account of the formulation of public health policy in antebellum Massachusetts.[28] The formation of the Massachusetts Board of Health in 1869 was the culmination of a complex effort involving physicians, interested citizens, and legislators. The first component of the process was the forging of a consensus that "the state is responsible for controlling disease, grounded on the normative view that public and personal health are...the birthright of Americans."[29] This essentially political proposition was based on more fundamental premises about society and disease: (1) that endemic and epidemic disease, rather than being a visitation from God, could and should be prevented; (2) that the causes of endemic and epidemic disease could be indentified by a variety of social and scientific criteria; and (3) that based on an understanding of these criteria, steps could and should be taken to prevent them. While these premises seem obvious to us, they were by no means generally accepted in the eighteenth century. As late as 1721, Bostonians rioted against those proposing smallpox inoculation and attempted to assassinate Cotton Mather, one of the most vocal proponents of the procedure.[30] Benjamin Franklin, then apprenticed to his brother, the publisher of the *New England Courant*, was one of the bitterest critics of those proposing inoculation (although he changed his mind on the subject after his son, Francis, died of the disease in 1736).[31] Opposition to the practice continued to be widespread until well after the Revolution: in 1776, a mob burned down the inoculation hospital at Cat Island and tarred and feathered four of its inhabitants; in the 1780s, the citizens of Middletown, Connecticut— then the largest city in the state—repeatedly declined to permit the erection of a "pock house" in the town.[32] Not until the 1790s were preventive measures against smallpox widely accepted.

The process through which the moral consensus involving the preventability of smallpox was forged is an interesting one—even though it is quite subsidiary to the issues which Rosenkrantz addresses. Ironically, opposition to inoculation was spearheaded not by the ministry (in spite of the opposition's use of theological justifications), but by anticlerical politicians and a handful of physicians.[33] In the 1720s, when inoculation was first introduced, there was no organized medical profession in America: most healing was done by physicians who practiced medicine as a sideline. There was, in other words, no organized enterprise through which the idea of disease prevention could be legitimated and spread. Between 1721 and the 1760s, the number of physicians in New England increased dramatically, primarily in response to the institutional crisis of the period.[34] Because ministers could not hand their pulpits down to their sons and because, in any event, the number of pulpits was limited, many ministers began to train their sons as physicians, since physic was one of the marketable skills they possessed.

By the 1760s, medical practice, especially in the towns and cities, had become highly competitive, and the first moves began to be made to create professional societies—organizations whose primary purpose was to limit the number of persons practicing medicine in any given place. The legislatures stoutly resisted these efforts, however, recognizing accurately that chartering the medical societies in the form described in the doctors' petitions would involve creating professional monopolies, which would be politically indefensible since physicians at that point lacked reputable credentials.

In the years between the 1760s and the 1790s, this situation was altered. First, formal institutional medical training began to be initiated—in the 1760s at the Pennsylvania Hospital, in the 1770s at King's College

(Columbia), and in the 1780s at Harvard. The creation of a recognized credential—a degree—which differentiated college-trained physicians from those who merely practiced healing was an important step towards professional legitimation. Second, as members of the profession came increasingly to be recruited from elite mercantile and ministerial families, physicians began to garner the family connections necessary to enhance their status as an occupational group and the political clout to make their interests heard in the legislature. Third, a major faction in the medical profession made concerted efforts to explicitly tie their interests to those of the economically and politically powerful; in both Massachusetts and Connecticut, for example, Federalist physicians made it clear to their political allies that chartering medical societies and tying them to the colleges through the establishment of medical schools would give their party control of the profession. Fourth, the Revolution had done much to popularize ideas about the perfectibility of man and society. This protoscientific ideology did much to lend credibility to the physicians' organizational efforts.

When the new procedure of vaccination against smallpox was introduced to New England in 1802, it was very differently received than inoculation had been eighty years before.[35] In 1799, Benjamin Waterhouse, a practicing physician and Professor of the Theory and Practice of Physic in the Harvard Medical School, received the first report of Edward Jenner's new method for preventing smallpox. After writing a brief description of the procedure for one of Boston's popular newspapers, he took the report to a meeting of the American Academy of Arts and Sciences, an organization of wealthy and influential politicians, professionals, and merchants which had been founded in 1783. The gentlemen of the Academy were "deeply interested" and with their implicit support, Waterhouse began a set of experimental tests of the procedure at a private smallpox hospital in Brookline, outside of Boston. When vaccination proved itself to be dramatically successful, Waterhouse communicated his findings to his colleagues in the Massachusetts Medical Society (chartered in 1780), to the American Academy, to President Jefferson, to the popular press, and to the Boston Board of Health. With endorsements from the Medical Society, the Academy, and Thomas Jefferson, the Board was willing to be persuaded to permit Waterhouse to build a smallpox hospital on Noddle's Island in Boston Harbor for the purpose of further testing vaccination. Nineteen boys were chosen as guinea pigs, were vaccinated and, within a few months, were brought in contact with live smallpox matter. Throughout this procedure, the subjects were examined by a group of six physicians who were to report on their progress to the Board of Health and to the Medical Society. On the strength of their endorsement, the Board pronounced itself convinced that cowpox vaccination provided complete security against smallpox. And with its decision, vaccination against smallpox became a generally accepted practice throughout New England.

The process through which the prevention of smallpox became an accepted practice between 1720 and 1802 represents only the first step in the process of public policy formulation—the step of consensus formation. Nevertheless, it reveals the crucial role of voluntary associations, even very early in American history, in defining issues (smallpox as a *disease* rather than a moral visitation), in shaping their perception (smallpox as a medical problem whose solution required medical intervention), and in forming power coalitions (ties between physicians, ties between physicians and influential economic and political actors, and the endorsement of prestigious medical and nonmedical institutions). At this stage, in spite of the importance of private voluntary associations, private philanthropy played only a small role in the process. Harvard still received significant, though declining, public support through the last decades of the eighteenth century and the early decades of the nineteenth (between 1760 and 1825, 37 percent of the university's revenue came from public sources), and state officials still sat on its governing boards.[36] The major professorships in the Harvard Medical School were the products of private endowments: the professorships of anatomy and surgery, chemistry, and theory and practice of physic were provided for under the wills of the Hersey and Erving families.[37] The Massachusetts Medical Society and the American Academy of Arts and Sciences, while operating entities, were supported by membership fees rather than endowment income or significant donations. However, in the later phases of establishing public health policy, philanthropically supported private voluntary bodies would play a much more central role.

The decades between 1800 and 1869, when the Commonwealth of Massachusetts finally established a Board of Health and began to define and implement public health policy on a state-wide basis, necessarily built on earlier conceptual and organizational achievements. Once again, consensus lay at the foundation of the effort. While Waterhouse had demonstrated the preventability of smallpox through an acceptable procedure and, in so doing, had convinced public authorities that physicians could be safely allowed to practice vaccination, this was still a long way from the creation of a public health policy, for vaccination remained a matter of individual choice and was administered for a price by private physicians. Although antebellum New England abounded with reformist schemes of every sort, the movement to create a public health policy proceeded haltingly. The major impediment to its development was the tendency of reformers to view disease as a reflection of the individual's moral condition: just as an individual could avoid the dangers of alcohol through good morals and self-discipline, so he could avoid the hazards of disease by the practice of "hygienic prophylaxis," i.e., by clean living. In spite of this moralistic and individualistic approach to the problem of public health, there was a clear and growing recognition that both the state and private organizations had a positive obligation to gather and disseminate the information that would enable individuals to better their condition. Beginning in the 1830s, men like Lemuel Shattuck, founder of the American Statistical Association, and physician Leonard Jarvis worked actively to promote the gathering of accurate quantitative data on both population and mortality and morbidity in the state. By the 1840s, with the help of the Statistical Association and the Massachusetts Medical Society, they had persuaded the state to adopt a uniform system of registering vital statistics and initiated a series of state-funded "sanitary surveys" to assess the condition of public health in Massachusetts.

But the real breakthrough for the formulation of public health policy did not come until the 1860s:

> During the Civil War, belief that susceptibility to disease could be diminished by specific intervention suggested a new role for medical authority. Evidence that personal hygiene could be guided and supplemented by scientific knowledge was reinforced by the efforts [promoted by a private body, the United States Sanitary Commission] to improve health in the army camps and hospitals. Beneficial effects were observed following the practice of boiling contaminated water, the prescription of sunlight and ventilation as a source of health, and the assignment of physicians to responsible army and hospital posts, all of which contributed to the recognition that it was possible to curtail disease. Although the filth theory of disease continued to be the basis for etiological concepts, public hygiene and personal health required the application of social as well as individual controls.[38]

Gradually, it came to be recognized that while statistics were useful—inasmuch as they described the incidence of mortality and morbidity and its correlation with a variety of social, economic, and environmental factors—they were also limited, for they shed no light on either etiology or prevention. As Dr. George Derby pointed out in an 1868 speech to the Boston Social Science Association, the possibilities for the prevention of specific diseases lay

> in the *advance of medical science,* which has given to physicians a better knowledge of the nature of disease, derived from careful observation of cases, and from modern discoveries in chemistry and physiology.[39]

What Derby asserted in 1868 became progressively clearer in the years that followed, as the advance of science demonstrated the role of microorganisms in the spread of disease and the importance of highly specialized sanitary and social engineering techniques in combating them. As this occurred, the major issues of public health concern came increasingly to depend on the judgments of qualified experts—engineers, chemists, physicians, biologists, and social scientists.

It was not coincidental that the decision of the Massachusetts legislature to establish the State Board of Health was preceded by intensive organizational activity in the private voluntary sector, fueled by a dramatic upsurge in private philanthropy. Harvard and the Massachusetts General Hospital, with which it was closely associated, were the major beneficiaries of private benevolence in the years following the Civil War. The university received $3.3 million in gifts and bequests between 1865 and 1885—more than doubling its capital and current gifts over the previous two decades.[40] These donations included funds for the establishment of two endowed chairs in anatomy, a professorship in pathological anatomy, and a professorship in clinical medicine (to supplement the three endowed chairs created when the medical school was established in the 1780s). Massachusetts General Hospital, which received $483,993 in gifts and donations between its founding in 1811 and 1851, more than doubled its philanthropic revenues over the next twenty years.[41] Not surprisingly, the Harvard-MGH complex proved to be—until the rise of Johns Hopkins in the 1880s—the major center of medical innovation in the United States, introducing nonpunitive "moral treatment" for the mentally ill (1818), pioneering the use of general anesthesia (1846), and understanding the etiology of purpureal fever (1847). After the war, with the election of Charles W. Eliot as Harvard's president, the pace of innovation quickened as Harvard became the first medical school in the United States to offer its students instruction in pathology, pathological anatomy, and embryology.[42]

While advancing scientific medical technology, the Harvard-MGH complex was also active in bringing those medical innovations to the public, not only through the dissemination of medical intelligence in the *Boston Medical and Surgical Journal* (now the *New England Journal of Medicine*), but also through making its facilities available to the poor (by 1872, an endowment of more than $154,000 supported free beds for the poor at the hospital).[43] Although MGH was not the only hospital in Boston by the 1870s, Harvard's influence extended well beyond it to such specialized private hospitals as the Perkins Institution for the Blind and the Massachusetts Eye and Ear Infirmary, as well as such major public institutions as the Boston City Hospital. No one concerned with public health could be immune to Harvard's overwhelming influence.

Not surprisingly, Harvard's influence was decisive in the formulation of public health policy in Massachusetts. In addition to its long-term role in upgrading the status of the medical profession, in establishing channels of communication between health professionals, and in sponsoring and making available advances in medical technology, the university played a key role in the political struggle to establish a state board of health and to define its purposes. The two foremost spokesmen for a coherent public policy on health and for the central role of expertise in its formulation were members of the Harvard faculty—Henry Ingersoll Bowditch, Jackson Professor of Clinical Medicine, and George Derby, Lecturer and Professor of Hygiene—both of whom ended up as members of the first health board. The board consisted of seven members: a journalist, two businessmen, a lawyer, and three physicians. The third physician member, although not a member of the Harvard faculty, had received his medical education there and was, like his colleagues Bowditch and Derby, an active member of the Massachusetts Medical Society and a leading lobbyist for public health legislation. He was an active politician as well, having served in the state senate and as a member of the United States Congress. Although a minority on the board, the physicians immediately assumed leadership. Bowditch was elected its first chairman and Derby its secretary.

The Massachusetts Board of Health as originally constituted did not meet the high expectations of its promoters. Since it had no executive authority, it could do little more than conduct investigations and make recommendations to local health departments. Nevertheless, as discoveries in the field of bacteriology established with ever greater clarity the specific causes of epidemic disease and as the medical profession itself became both more scientific in its orientation (thanks in large part to Eliot's reform of the Harvard Medical School) and more politically aggressive, an alliance began to develop between the advocates of a more powerful state health board—with the ability to define and enforce sanitary codes—and the civil service reformers, who sought to replace the patronage system of officeholding with merit appointments. By the late 1880s, this goal was largely achieved as the state assumed a permanent and ongoing responsibility for public health; its decisions were shaped by medical, engineering, and social intelligence largely generated in the private sector from the university—hospital—professional society complex and enforced by a staff recruited and trained in the private sector.

How important was private philanthropy in the development of public health policy in nineteenth-century Massachusetts? It appears to have been crucial. While many physicians continued to be trained by apprenticeship until almost the end of the century, those who were trained in medical schools—at Harvard, Bowdoin, Dartmouth, and the Berkshire Medical Institution—were clearly the most influential members of the profession. All these medical schools were private. All were supported by a private philanthropy that enabled them to become centers of medical intelligence (through the creation of medical libraries, the publication of journals, and the establishment of prize competitions), medical innovation (through the funding of laboratories and the purchase of experimental apparatus), and medical influence (through the educational and professional process serving both as a networking device between physicians and for the creation of ties between physicians and powerful economic and political forces in the state). Although Massachusetts was a pioneer in the establishment of such publicly-funded health facilities as the Worcester State Hospital (1832), priorities of state institutions tended to be set by the privately organized medical profession. At no time did the state itself take the lead in initiating innovation in medicine or public health.

Those states which had placed obstacles in the way of private philanthropy—including New York and the Southern states—were notably backward as sources of both medical innovation and public health measures. Although New York's physicians tried repeatedly through the early years of the nineteenth century to create a system of health inspection and to define the public responsibility for the health of the community, their efforts were continually hampered by politics. As George Rosen noted in his *History of Public Health:*

> Cornelius B. Archer. . .succeeded in 1853 in having enacted an improved Birth, Marriage, and Death Registration Act. Nevertheless, the administrative machinery available was intolerably inefficient. For one thing, these positions were much sought after, and political machinations played a considerable role in the filling of the posts. As a result, officials were often subject to political influence, and in numerous instances were highly incompetent.[44]

The New York of William Marcy Tweed and his mentors was hardly an ideal setting for defining or implementing public health policy! But the physicians and other supporters of sanitary reform might have carried the day if they had enjoyed sufficient influence.

Boston, like all big cities, was also politically corrupt. But, thanks largely to the concentration of philanthropic giving on a handful of closely interlocked institutions, the medical community was remarkably unified. This was not the case in New York, however, where medical schools, for-profit and nonprofit, as well as rival medical societies struggled continually for dominance. As Philadelphia physician Benjamin Rush wrote to his New York colleague David Hosack in 1812:

> Let us show the world that a difference of medical opinion upon medical subjects is not incompatible with medical friendships; and in so doing, let us throw the whole odium of hostility of physicians to each other upon their competition for business and money. Alas! while merchants, mechanics, lawyers, and the clergy live in a friendly intercourse with each other. . .physicians in all ages and countries riot upon one anothers' characters.[45]

Without prestige or unified financial, technical, and political resources, the physicians were insufficiently powerful to resist the politicization of public health agencies. Not until 1864 were physicians in the city able to carry out a thorough survey of sanitary conditions in New York, finally doing so under the auspices of a private group, the Council of Hygiene and Public Health, which was part of the main umbrella organization promoting the reform of municipal government, the Citizens Association of New York.[46] The findings of the report led the New York State legislature to establish a Metropolitan Board of Health in 1866, a move that owed more to the ongoing warfare between state and city governments than to any strong convictions about public well-being. (The state had in 1857 established a Metropolitan police force—under the governor's control—

to do battle with the constabulary appointed by the city's Democratic machine.)[47] In any event, the board was not able to operate free of political influence until after 1872, when Tweed and his henchmen were ousted from their positions of influence. Even with the board in operation, sanitary conditions in New York remained far from salubrious, as Jacob Riis's *How the Other Half Lives* (1890) would eloquently testify.[48] Only in the 1890s, when the legislature removed obstacles to private philanthropy, were Columbia and the city's private hospitals enabled to become recipients of large scale benevolence (which was paralleled, not coincidently, by the incorporation of the College of Physicians and Surgeons into the University),[49] and not until after the turn of the century would New York possess the institutional mechanisms for articulating and endorcing a modern public health policy.

Public Policy and Philanthropy in the Twentieth Century: Progressivism, Professionalism, and the Institutional System of Modern Liberalism

Until thirty years ago, Progressivism was regarded as a *political* movement involving the divergence of the business-oriented Republican "Old Guard" represented by such men as Marcus Alonzo Hanna (the Republican boss behind William McKinley and William Howard Taft), and the younger aggressively reformist element led by Theodore Roosevelt. The historiography of the past thirty years, most notably the work of Richard Hofstadter, Robert Weibe, and Burton Bledstein, dramatically broadened our understanding of Progressivism.[50] It is now generally seen as a cultural movement with profound political, social, and economic implications.

The basic constituency of the movement is now understood to be the generation of men and women educated in the newly reformed American universities between 1870 and 1910.[51] Their educational experiences appear to have produced in them a set of values which, while drawing on the past, were also a dramatic departure from it. They saw a particular value in specialized expertise, i.e., in professionalism. Vocational specialization did not, however, lead them away from organizational activity. Because organizational activity was inextricably bound to an ideal of service—and because their historical experience made it plain that social, economic, and political achievement was collective rather than individual in nature—they were oriented toward working through hierarchical collectivities. This "new middle class," as Robert Weibe called them, were the group that reorganized American life on a bureaucratic basis.

But to characterize the organizational orientation of the Progressive generation as bureaucratic is to oversimplify and reify a complex process involving both persons and institutions. These individuals did not merely set out to create administrative hierarchies within particular institutions. The power of bureaucratic organization rested not merely on the employment of experts and the subdivision and hierarchical ordering of tasks.

Rather, it depended on an ongoing set of relationships between the institutions that produced knowledge and trained manpower and those that used them, i.e., between universities, business corporations, and professional organizations. The survival of the modern business corporations that emerged into the intensely competitive national and international markets of the late nineteenth and early twentieth centuries required continuous access to basic science and technology, as well as continuous improvements in the social and quantitative intelligence that would enable corporate managers to produce and distribute goods on a mass scale.

But bureaucratization involved more than the establishment of institutional systems within the private for-profit and nonprofit sectors. It inevitably reached out to the public sector as well. There are several reasons for this. First, the service ethos of the Progressives, coming as it did out of the experience of Civil War and Reconstruction, was always publicly oriented, as Charles W. Eliot and the other reform-minded educators who trained the generation made clear.[52] Second, the economic and social turbulence of the years 1873 to 1894 made clear not only the need for order in the private sector (through such devices as industrial trusts) but also the extent to which private actions invariably had public consequences which could not be ignored. Third, the bureaucratizers from the mid-1880s on had to respond to a set of explicitly political challenges to their efforts to reorganize American life. As industrial and cultural life became increasingly consolidated, Populists and other radicals mounted programs and proposed legislation to curtail the power of the private sector: by the 1870s, the tax exemption for private charities was under attack in a number of states; the virtual private monopoly of higher education was being threatened by the new state universities and by proposals to establish a national institution of higher learning; antitrust legislation, the creation of regulatory agencies, and proposals for subtreasury and monetary schemes all threatened the autonomy of the private sector.

The Progressives did not, it should be pointed out, oppose government action *per se*. Indeed, reformers had championed such regulatory efforts as boards of health and charity and railroad commissions. But they were acutely aware of the hazards of big government in the hands of the politically corrupt. Yet by the turn of the century, when the success of civil service reform efforts on the local, state, and federal levels seemed assured, and when the professional experts became convinced that their counsels would be listened to by those holding political office, the Progressive generation began to organize politically—not as a new political party, but as an increasingly powerful faction within both parties.

It would be a mistake to suppose, as some historians have, that the Progressive thrust was narrowly based on the energies of professionals (at least as that term is generally construed). While physicians, lawyers, clergymen, engineers, and intellectuals were undoubtedly important elements in the

Progressive coalition, their effectiveness was inextricably linked to the sympathy and financial support of significant elements in the business community and, in particular, to the growing importance of the first generation of professional managers—men like Alfred P. Sloan, Gerard Swope, and Walter S. Gifford—who were beginning to take control of American industry.[53] Progressivism became an effective political force because of its ability to attract the professional and managerial specialists and to tap the financial and informational resources of the private sector over which they presided.

The consolidation and politicization of a national managerial elite within the private sector did not, however, lead inevitably either to political power or to an ability to formulate and implement public policy. To begin with, the private sector itself was far from monolithic; even the large private universities varied enormously in quality and resources, and large business corporations operated at cross-purposes and with varying levels of efficiency and public responsibility. Further, even if private institutions had been more or less unified in their goals and methods, political power still required an ability to influence the voting public. As they began to cohere politically in the first decade of the twentieth century, the Progressives faced monumental tasks of unifying the private sector and influencing the public.

To a certain extent, events played into their hands. While reformers had long been concerned about such issues as food adulteration, and had written on the subject for years, they could hardly have counted on the national reponse to Upton Sinclair's 1906 novel, *The Jungle*. In fact, Sinclair, a socialist who had written the book to call attention to the miserable working and living conditions of immigrants, lamented after his book's success that he had aimed the book "at the nation's heart but hit its stomach."[54] That the public and politicians responded to *The Jungle* as an exposé of food adulteration rather than of poverty had much to do with the character of powerful organized professional groups. Organized medicine, as well as popular journalists, had been hammering on the theme of food impurities for decades. In certain states there were already policies in place to deal with the problem, which was a good indication that the first steps of public policy formulation—the creation of a moral consensus defining it is an appropriate arena for state action and the perceptual shaping defining it as a problem in medicine and chemistry—had already been taken. As early as 1902, Dr. Harvey Washington Wiley (B.S. Harvard, 1873), Chief Chemist of the Department of Agriculture, had been quietly investigating food impurities and their effects. President Roosevelt (B.A. Harvard, 1879) had, from his experience as Police Commissioner of New York and as an officer in the Spanish-American War, an awareness of the dangers of adulteration. Even before the publication of Sinclair's book, he had begun drafting federal legislation to deal with the problem. But the publication of *The Jungle* acted as a catalyst, focusing public attention on a set of problems that had already been defined by privately supported agencies as public in nature and scientific in their solution. The rapidity with which Roosevelt was able to get a Pure Food and Drug Law passed, establishing mechanisms for articulating and enforcing policy, was a testament less to Sinclair's book than to the commitment of philanthropic dollars over the years to creating agricultural chemistry as a field and to training men like Dr. Wiley and his assistants.

But private philanthropy's most important contribution to Progressivism and to the establishment of a public policy process lay not in areas of specialized scientific, medical, or engineering expertise, but in the ability of the state to deal with the broadest issues of social and economic organization. This kind of policy making required *social intelligence*, i.e., methods for gathering and interpreting information about the behavior and attitudes of large groups. This enterprise stemmed from a number of sources, almost all of which were the products of private benevolence. One group, already noted, consisted of statisticians like the sanitarians Lemuel Shattuck and Leonard Jarvis. It also included men like Henry Varnum Poor, who viewed the quantitative analysis of business firms as a key to more comprehensive reforms in society.[55] These men were linked to another important group consisting of reform-minded businessmen, many of whom were members of such organizations as the American Social Science Association and the American Statistical Association.[56] These businessmen had the means to underwrite the early development of the academic study of economic and social relations, and politics. It was under such auspices that the social sciences began to be studied at Harvard when, in 1868, a group of businessmen led by investment banker Henry Lee began giving annual gifts for lectures in "political economy."[57]

By political economy, these business philanthropists did not mean the old-style philosophical approach taught by old-timers like Francis Bowen, Harvard's Professor of Religion, Moral Philosophy, and Civil Polity. They were interested in funding "lectures on the practical affairs of business, and the relations between labor and capital."[58] And they wanted it taught not from the works of philosophers like John Stuart Mill, but from more practical texts. Because there were no academically trained economists in the United States, Harvard's first instructor in political economy was Charles F. Dunbar, whose training for the job consisted of two decades on the staff—and ultimately as the editor—of Boston's major financial newspaper, *The Boston Advertiser*.[59] The social sciences at Yale and Columbia had similar beginnings. William Graham Sumner, Yale's first instructor in political economy, was closely tied to the Young Yale movement, an organization of New York business alumni who, from the late 1860s on, worked to wrest control of the university from the Connecticut clergymen who had controlled the institution since its foundation.[60] Similarly, Columbia's Faculty of Political Science was the fruit of efforts led by New York businessman Samuel Ruggles.[61]

Another factor in the development of the social sciences was religious, originating particularly among the clergy and laity who had, on the one hand, become sensitized to the poverty and social disorder of the nation's growing cities, and, on the other, were sufficiently cosmopolitan to be aware of the formulation of the Social Gospel in England. Although ethically motivated, American Social Gospellers like Harvard's Francis Greenwood Peabody advocated a pragmatic approach to social problems based first and foremost on the kinds of social survey techniques that had been pioneered in England by Charles Booth.[62] Not content to observe and analyze, Peabody was a leader in tying the academic study of social problems to social action by channeling students into social service activities. By the turn of the century, over 400 Harvard students were engaged in volunteer social work.

Although it stemmed from a variety of sources, the social science enterprise coalesced by the 1880s, producing a group of academic professional organizations, many of which, like the American Economic Association and the American Statistical Association, continued to include influential laymen from the business community. These became the basis not only for the systematic gathering and analysis of social, economic, and political data (followed by publication in the new scholarly journals distributed by the professional organizations), but also for the production of a cadre of academic specialists who would take their places in the colleges and universities that were following the lead of the elite private institutions in reforming their curricula. More important than this, however, was the role of the elective undergraduate curriculum, through which countless young people came to be sensitized to the social science approach before going on to make careers in business and government—and to serve as community leaders. These individuals would be the creators of "welfare capitalism," which would promote not only the formation of trade associations, the major lobbying groups in the economic policy process, but also the early programs of corporate responsibility that would, by World War I, make business a major actor in the realm of private charity.[63]

The development of the enterprise of social intelligence was only a preliminary to the emergence of organizations whose explicit purpose was the formulation of public policy: the general purpose charitable foundations and the public policy research institutions. While the earliest endowments resembling modern foundations date from the years immediately following the Civil War—the Peabody and Slater Funds—their focus was more specifically educational and more explicitly directed to defined groups of beneficiaries than the focus of the foundations established after the turn of the century would be. Even Andrew Carnegie's 1904 endowment, the Carnegie Institution of Washington, while highly flexible in its purposes, influenced policy only indirectly by funding particular endeavors in the social and natural sciences.[64]

But the Russell Sage Foundation, which would combine the features of both the general purpose foundation and the policy research institute, represented a new mechanism for the formulation of public policy. Established in 1907 by Margaret Olivia Slocum Sage, the foundation was very much tied to the previous four decades of ferment in the closely-linked worlds of philanthropy and academic social science. Although an active philanthropist herself, Mrs. Sage's decision to create a perpetual endowment "for improvement of social and living conditions in the United States" was molded by her legal advisors, Robert and Henry DeForest.[65] Both Yale graduates whose careers at the university coincided with William Graham Sumner's years there, the DeForest brothers had taken an active role in such organizations as the New York Charity Organization Society and the National Conference of Charities and Correction. By 1900, they had come to share in the conviction—so articulately expressed by another Darwinian philanthropist, Andrew Carnegie—that charitable funds would be most effectively applied not in the amelioration of human misery, but in its *prevention*. Robert DeForest looked to the academic study of social problems as a source of preventative action. And it was through his influence that the first head of the foundation was John M. Glenn, a protege of Daniel Coit Gilman, the first president of Johns Hopkins (who was also founder of the Baltimore Charity Organization Society and first president of the Carnegie Institution of Washington). The major thrust of the foundation was to be the consolidation of the decentralized social research effort, the publication of important results, and the funding of innovative new work in the field. One of the foundation's most important early efforts, the five-year Pittsburgh Survey (1907-1912), had the explicit purpose of "providing accurate measures of social conditions," making them available to influential members of the community, and, by this means, mobilizing public opinion to change social and economic conditions.[66] By the second decade of the twentieth century, activities funded by the Sage Foundation had set a pattern through which public policy came to be made cooperatively by *technical experts*, usually from the universities (who generated the information deliniating problems and suggesting their solutions), interested *private citizens* (usually strategically situated graduates of elite private universities), and *governments* (which, because of the electoral success of university graduates, as well as major reforms in municipal law and administration, were steadily less dominated by old-time political machines).[67]

It would be redundant to recount the tale of the formation of the Rockefeller philanthropies, the Brookings Institution, the Twentieth Century Fund, the National Bureau of Economic Research, and the host of other endowed policy-oriented organizations of the Progressive Era. The important thing is to understand their role in the policy process. For, from the beginning of the century, governments on all levels depended less and less on the "will of the electorate" as expressed by political leaders and the press. As the problems with which governments dealt became increasingly complex and amenable only to technical analysis, governments at all levels tended to depend on the institutional system of universities, professional and academic disciplines, foundations, and policy research institutes for solutions. In so doing, governments became increasingly *policy oriented*, creating legislation to deal with major social and economic issues not as a series of isolated acts, but as a coherent, rationalized, and information-based system of ideas implemented by trained cadres of technically proficient officials.

Until the recent blooming of historiographical interest in the 1920s, it was generally assumed that the bureaucratic, policy-oriented state was a creation of Franklin Roosevelt's New Deal. The work of Ellis Hawley, Joan Hoff Wilson, Louis Galambos, and others has made it clear that Big Government had its roots in the pre-World War I years and its first flowering in the 1920s under the leadership of Herbert Hoover.[68] What is not clear, however, is the relative influence of the public and private sectors in the formulation of state policy. For the simultaneous growth of government's social and economic activism and the rise of policy-oriented philanthropy—as well as the ubiquity of individuals whose career lines pass through both institutional sectors— makes it virtually impossible to differentiate the two. The modern public and private organizational system is an institutional hybrid of both. And determining where one begins and the other ends is probably the major task facing organizational historians and theorists in the next decade.

Hybridization notwithstanding, I would be willing to advance the notion that private philanthropy was—and still remains—a major force in shaping both the moral consensus on which public policy is based and the perception from which the definition and solution of problems proceeds. Although the federal government began to be a significant factor in the funding of research during and after World War II, its funding activities, funneled through such agencies as the National Science Foundation, the National Institutes of Health, and, by the 1960s, the endowments for the arts and the humanities, were more influenced by priorities set in the universities (the most important of which remained private institutions) and in the academic professions (which were organized as private nonprofit entities) than by politics. Indeed, it was the assurance that these agencies would remain free of political control (and also, perhaps, of the political influence of leading academics) that gave them public legitimacy. With their creation, the federal government began for the first time to develop a policy formation capacity comparable to that of the private sector. But as long as a private sector policy "establishment" remained intact, there was no rivalry between public and private sources of policy.

In the 1960s, this cooperative public—private pattern began to change. One factor in this was the passing of the old Progressive generation of policy makers—the Robert Morse Lovetts, the Dulleses, the James Bryant Conants. No less important was the shattering of the bipartisan social and foreign policy consensus that had defined legislative options since the late 1930s—a casualty of the Vietnam War and the civil rights movement.[69] Finally, the New Right (bearer of the Jacksonian/Populists tradition in American political life) began to move from being "a set of irritable gestures which pass for thought" to an organized political force complete with its own foundations, philanthropic priorities, and policy research institutes. Although rhetorically favoring private sector over state action, the New Right did not dismantle the policy machinery of the Progressive/Liberal state. It politicized it and made it more sensitive to legislative pressure. Beginning with the Nixon administration, the National Science Foundation and the Institutes of Health began determining their research and grant-giving priorities along political lines, underwriting research activities ("such as a war on cancer") that could be counted on to yield political and public relations benefits. At the same time, the projects funded by government began to be the subject of explicit political comment (as with Senator Proxmire's "Golden Fleece Awards").

Private philanthropy has only begun to adjust to the impact of the break up of liberalism and the Reagan Revolution. Ironically, the strictures on political advocacy by nonprofit organizations imposed in the 1969 tax reform act and in subsequent legislation have reduced the flexibility with which institutionalized philanthropy might have responded to the policy shift. At the same time, as the work of Lester Salamon and Alan Abramson has made clear, cutbacks in federal social expenditures have affected the private nonprofit sector far more profoundly than anyone would have guessed before 1980. For, as their analyses have shown, the government itself had become one of the largest sources of revenue for private eleemosynary organizations.[70] Government spending cutbacks thus not only demanded a higher level of activity from private charity, but also reduced the revenues available to compensate for reductions in state services.

It remains to be seen whether the federal government will curtail its social expenditure to the extent originally promised by the Reagan administration. The likelihood of the private sector being able to take up the resulting slack in social services remains unclear. What has become clear, however, is the necessity under which private philanthropy is now laboring to redefine its public role. While most of this activity focuses on specific areas—the relative cost, efficiency, and adequacy of public versus private health care facilities, for example—perhaps the most significant work involves explorations to the framework of policy making and implementation itself, such as that undertaken by Alan Pifer and Forrest Chisman.[71] Not only are the organizations of the nonprofit sector drawing together to analyze their own past and prospects through such entities as the Council on Foundations and Independent Sector, but there also is significant scholarly activity both in the universities and in privately funded research institutes whose purpose is to explore the past and delineate the future of the private sector in the policy process.

A Personal Speculation on Private Philanthropy and Public Policy

As a historian, I am reluctant to speculate on the directions in which this work will lead. On the one hand, the consensus that there should be such a thing as public policy and that the state is the most appropriate vehicle for implementing it seems to be broadly intact—embracing even the New Right itself. On the other hand, the nature of the organizations that will shape the moral consensus, the perception, and the definition of public policy concerns has yet to be clarified. I personally think it unlikely that the Progressive/Liberal institutional system (and the pro-scientific professional consensus that underlay it) will be reassembled—at least in the foreseeable future. This should not be taken to suggest that private philanthropy will be deprived of its public influence but, rather, that its impact will be felt on other levels and through new mechanisms.

Two areas seem to offer particular promise. The first is the community foundation movement, through which the charitable resources of localities and regions are coming to be consolidated and rationalized. Because the results of charity given locally are more immediately obvious and because local donor constituencies are more able to exert control over how their gifts are used, I believe that we are going to see not only more philanthropy focused in this direction, but also a more active policy role on the local level. As federal influence diminishes along with federal funding, local groups will be more and more likely to see to it that both their philanthropic and their tax dollars are more effectively used. And the concentrated resources of the private sector are likely to profoundly influence this process. Second, my experience as a volunteer in local nonprofits and in local government suggests that philanthropic energies and resources may find distinctly local foci. These will take two forms: (1) the formation of local bodies with explicit policy formulating purposes; and (2) the formation of privately funded alternatives to government and for-profit agencies.

I have already seen the influence of private locally-directed policy organizations on the public policies of local government. Because of public distrust of the municipality (a well-founded distrust based on the domination of the town boards by a particularly venial political machine), the voters of the town in which I live had repeatedly turned down efforts to redevelop its deteriorated commercial core. Three years ago, however, a group of local merchants, realtors, developers, architects, and planners began holding a series of meetings to discuss the future of "downtown." Funded by private donations, by small contributions from the municipality (whose leadership had by then begun to pass to anti-machine forces), and by contributions from the newly formed community foundation, the group eventually drafted a comprehensive planning document which detailed not only what was to be done, but how—including the relative contributions of the municipality, the merchants, and potential developers. The plan is now being implemented, and with remarkable success. I am in no position to say how widespread cooperative public—private patterns of this kind are in the United States. But it is a matter worthy of investigation.

Thus far, the matter of alternatives to public agencies such as schools has largely been a matter of reactionary responses to desegregation orders. But my personal experience with the new breed of private schools and cooperative day-care enterprises suggests that private education in the Northeast is only decreasingly a function of the desire of the well-to-do to set themselves apart from the masses and more a serious effort by those interested in quality education to develop alternatives to the public schools. The motives driving many of the parents who support such efforts are worth examining. Most of the parents from my town who send their children to private schools not only believe in public education, but were leaders in the effort to persuade the municipality to retain neighborhood schools. When the political machine ignored their pleas, closed the local schools, and consolidated public education in a system whose quality was so poor that it was unable to obtain a regular state accreditation, they had little choice but to seek alternatives. The final irony is that the two private schools to which most of them sent their children are both more experimental pedagogically than the public schools (thus belying the suggestion that they are mere status mechanisms) and more racially and ethnically inclusive than the public schools—having substantial scholarship funds which are expended precisely for the purpose of providing a community service and making quality education accessible.

How typical these experiences are and, if they are typical, how they will aggregate is difficult to foresee. They do not point to an end for a national philanthropic focus, for one of the most interesting aspects of these local incidents is the extent to which the individuals involved have continued to draw on nationally generated sources of information and expertise. At the same time, they point to a major shift in the areas and constituencies which will be most benefited by private philanthropy, especially in its policy role.

NOTES

[1]Alexis de Tocqueville, *Democracy in America* (New York: The Modern Library, 1981), pp. 39-40.

[2]*ibid.*, pp. 403-404.

[3]*ibid.*, p. 105.

[4]On the centrality of the family in early American life, see Philip Greven, *Four Generations: Family, Land, and Population in Colonial Andover, Massachusetts* (Ithaca: Cornell University Press, 1970); Mary P. Ryan, *Cradle of the Middle Class: The Family in Oneida County, New York, 1790-1865* (New York: Cambridge University Press, 1981); and Peter Dobkin Hall, *The Organization of American Culture: Institutions, Elites, and the Origins of American Nationality* (New York: New York University Press, 1982).

[5]The best discussion of colonial apprenticeship is contained in Bernard Farber, *Guardians of Virtue: Salem Families in 1800* (New York: St. Martins Press, 1973).

[6]On the duties of the head of the housebold, see Edmund S. Morgan, *The Puritan Family* (New York: Harper & Row, 1966).

[7]P.D. Hall, *Organization of American Culture*, pp. 35-54.

[8]Curiously, there has been no comprehensive book-length treatment of poverty in early America. Sources on the subject include Edward M. Capen, *The Historical Development of the Poor Law of Connecticut* (New York: Columbia University Press, 1905); Douglas Lamar Jones, "The Strolling Poor: Transiency in Eighteenth Century Massachusetts," *Journal of Social History*, vol. 8 (Spring 1975); and David Rothaman, *Discovery of the Asylum: Social Order and Disorder in the New Republic* (Boston: Little, Brown & Company, 1971).

[9]Bruce C. Daniels, *The Connecticut Town* (Middletown: Wesleyan University Press, 1979).

[10]On kinship in Connecticut politics, see Edmund S. Morgan, *The Gentle Puritan—A Life of Ezra Stiles* (New Haven: Yale University Press, 1962).

[11]David D. Hall, *The Faithful Shepherd: A History of the New England Ministry in the Seventeenth Century* (New York: W.W. Norton & Company, 1972).

[12]Perhaps the most eloquent testimonial to this relationship is Benjamin Franklin's *Autobiography*. Virtually all of Franklin's pioneering associational activity involved young tradesmen like himself who, unlike earlier generations, were forced by circumstances to make it on their own. With the decline of patriarchal support systems, fraternalistic relations of mutual support such as the Junto were a reasonable alternative.

[13]Greven, *Four Generations*.

[14]The best account of this process of delegitimation is Richard Bushman, *From Puritan to Yankee: Character and the Social Order in Connecticut, 1690-1765* (New York: W.W. Norton & Company, 1970).

[15]On the familial rhetoric of the Foundation Fathers, see Winthrop D. Jordan, "Familial Politics: Thomas Paine and the Killing of the King, 1776," *Journal of American History*, vol. 60, no. 2 (September 1973), pp. 294-308; and John J. Waters, "James Otis, Jr.: An Ambivalent Revolutionary," *History of Childhood Quarterly*, vol. 1, no. 1 (Summer 1973), pp. 142-150.

[16]One of the most detailed accounts of the disillusionment of the Revolutionary idealists is Richard Rollins, *The Long Journey of Noah Webster* (Philadelphia: University of Pennsylvania Press, 1980).

[17]On the Federalist response to the Jeffersonian "revolution," see Richard Purcell, *Connecticut in Transition* (New Haven: Yale University Press, 1918); Noble Cunningham, *The Jeffersonian Republicans in Power: Party Operations, 1801-1809*

(Chapel Hill: University of North Carolina Press, 1963); and Paul Goodman, *The Democratic Republicans of Massachusetts* (Boston: Little, Brown & Company, 1964).

[18]Lyman Beecher, *A Plea for the West* (Cincinnati: Truman & Smith, 1835).

[19]On the evangelical counteroffensive, see P.D. Hall, *Organization of American Culture*, pp. 151-177; Charles I. Foster, *An Errand of Mercy: The Evangelical United Front, 1790-1837* (Chapel Hill: University of North Carolina Press, 1960); and David Allmendinger, *Paupers and Scholars: The Transformation of Student Life in Nineteenth Century New England* (New York: St. Martins Press, 1973). For detailed accounts of the relation between evangelicalism and associational activity in local contexts, see Ryan, *Cradle of the Middle Class*; and Paul Johnson, *Shopkeeper's Millenium* (New York: Hill & Wang, 1982).

[20]For a detailed account of the financing of early nonprofits, see Ronald Story, *The Forging of an Aristocracy: Harvard and Boston's Upper Class* (Middletown: Wesleyan University Press, 1980). An excellent account of the financial support for evangelicalism is contained in Whitney R. Cross, *The Burned Over District: The Social and Intellectual History of Enthusiastic Religion in Western New York, 1800-1850* (New York: Harper & Row, 1965).

[21]"Dartmouth College v. Woodward," 4 *Wheaton* 518 (1819).

[22]Dr. Burton, *To The Public: Priestcraft Exposed and Primitive Christianity Explained* (New York: Lockport, 1828).

[23]St. George Tucker, quoted in Howard Miller, *The Legal Foundations of American Philanthropy, 1776-1844* (Madison: The State Historical Society of Wisconsin, 1961), p. 25.

[24]James Barr Ames, "The Failure of the Tilden Trust," in *Lectures in Legal History* (Cambridge: Harvard University Press, 1913); and Austin Wakeman Scott, "Charitable Trusts in New York," *New York University Law Review*, vol. 26 (April 1951).

[25]For the relative growth of the endowments of the major private universities in the eighteenth and nineteenth centuries, see Jesse B. Sears, *Philanthropy and American Higher Education* (Washington, DC: Office of Education, 1923).

[26]For a discussion of the significance of these decisions, see P.D. Hall, *Organization of American Culture*, pp. 95-124.

[27]Samuel Atkins Eliot, "The Charities of Boston," *North American Review* (July 1860), pp. 149-165.

[28]Barbara G. Rosenkrantz, *Public Health and the State: Changing Views in Massachusetts, 1842-1936* (Cambridge: Harvard University Press, 1972).

[29]*ibid.*, p. 2.

[30]Ola Elizabeth Winslow, *A Destroying Angel: The Conquest of Smallpox in Colonial Boston* (Boston: Houghton Mifflin Company, 1974).

[31]Benjamin Franklin, *Autobiography and Other Writings* (New York: Signet Books, 1961), pp. 112, 284.

[32]Petitions from physicians requesting permission to erect facilities for inoculation during the period 1785-1800 are contained in the files of the Middletown, Connecticut City Clerk.

[33]Winslow, *Destroying Angel*, pp. 78-93.

[34]On the growth of the medical profession in New England, see Peter Dobkin Hall, "The Social Foundations of Professional Credibility: Linking the Medical Profession to Higher Education in Connecticut and Massachusetts, 1700-1830," Thomas Haskell, ed., *The Authority of Experts: Studies in History and Theory* (Bloomington: Indiana University Press, 1984), pp. 107-141; and Eric H. Christianson, "The Medical Practitioners of Massachusetts, 1630-1800," Philip Cash, et al., eds., *Medicine in Colonial Massachusetts* (Boston: Massachusetts Historical Society, 1980).

[35]Winslow, *Destroying Angel*, pp. 94-111; and L.E. Hawes, *Benjamin Waterhouse, M.D.* (Boston: Francis A. Countway Library of Medicine: 1974).

[36]On the changing relationship between Harvard and the state, see Story, *Forging of an Aristocracy*; and John S. Whitehead, *The Separation of College and State* (New Haven: Yale University Press, 1973).

[37]Harvard University, *Quinquennial Catalogue of Officers and Graduates* (Cambridge: Harvard University Press, 1936).

[38]Rosenkrantz, *Public Health and the State*, pp. 49-50.

[39]*ibid.*, p. 51.

[40]Sears, *Philanthropy*, p. 23.

[41]Summaries of gifts received by MGH are contained in N.I. Bowditch, *A History of the Massachusetts General Hospital* (Boston: Massachusetts General Hospital, 1872).

[42]Frederick C. Shattuck and J. Lewis Bremer, "The Medical School, 1869-1929," S.E. Morison, ed., *The Development of Harvard University Since the Inauguration of President Eliot* (Cambridge: Harvard University Press, 1930), pp. 555-602.

[43]Bowditch, *A History*, pp. 718-725.

[44]George Rosen, *A History of Public Health* (New York: MD Publications, Inc., 1958), p. 235.

[45]Quoted in Eric Labaree, *The Benevolent and Necessary Institution: New York Hospital* (New York: Doubleday, 1972), p. 174.

[46]Rosen, *History of Public Health*, pp. 244-248.

[47]Alexander Callow, *The Tweed Ring* (New York: Oxford University Press, 1965), pp. 146-147.

[48]Jacob A. Riis, *How the Other Half Lives: Studies Among the Tenements of New York* (New York: Charles Scribner's Sons, 1929).

[49]The dramatic impact of the 1893 reform of New York's charity laws is reflected in the flood of gifts and bequests received by Columbia University. Between 1750 and 1890, Columbia received a *total* of $465,460 in donations from individuals. Between 1890 and 1900, donations totaled $8,504,545. Sears, *Philanthropy*, p. 26.

[50]The key works redefining Progressivism are Richard Hofstadter, *Age of Reform* (New York: Alfred A. Knopf, 1955); Robert Weibe, *The Search for Order* (New York: Hill & Wang, 1967); and Burton J. Bledstein, *The Culture of Professionalism: The Middle Class and the Development of Higher Education in America* (New York: W.W. Norton & Company, 1976).

[51]Weibe, *Search for Order*, pp. 111-132; Bledstein, *Culture of Professionalism*, pp. 248-286.

[52]The most articulate early statement of the linkage between specialization and the ethos of service is contained in Charles W. Eliot's 1869 inaugural address as Harvard's president. Progressive era echoes of Eliot's sentiments include William James's "The Moral Equivalent of War" (1910) and Herbert Croly's *The Promise of American Life* (New York: The Macmillan Company, 1909). The latter was considered by Theodore Roosevelt to be the best summation of the Progressive credo. For an excellent discussion of the intellectual context of this linkage, see George M. Frederickson, *The Inner Civil War: Northern Intellectuals and the Crisis of the Union* (New York: Harper & Row, 1968), pp. 217-238.

[53]The most detailed examination of progressive thought in the business community is Morrill Heald, *The Social Responsibilities of Business: Corporation and Community, 1900-1960* (Cleveland: The Press of Case Western Reserve University, 1970). Also of interest is Robert Weibe's *Businessmen and Reform: A Study of the Progressive Movement* (Cambridge: Harvard University Press, 1962). I am currently engaged in a study of the social, political, and cultural activities of the 1870-1940 business graduates of Harvard, Yale, and Columbia. The patterns I find

substantiate the business/reform connection that I suggest here. See Peter Dobkin Hall, "Doing Well by Doing Good: Business Philanthropy and Social Investment, 1860-1984," Virginia Hodgkinson, ed., *Giving and Volunteering: New Frontiers of Knowledge* (Washington, D.C.: Independent Sector, 1984), pp. 27-73.

[54]On the response to *The Jungle*, see Henry Pringle, *Theodore Roosevelt: A Biography* (New York: Harcourt, Brace & World, Inc., 1956). Useful accounts of the politics of the regulation under Roosevelt include John M. Blum, *The Republican Roosevelt* (New York: Atheneum, 1965), pp. 73-105; and George E. Mowry, *The Era of Theodore Roosevelt and the Birth of Modern America* (New York: Harper & Row, 1962), pp. 197-225.

[55]On Poor's reformist motives, see Alfred D. Chandler, "Henry Varnum Poor: Philosopher of Management, 1812-1905," William Miller, ed., *Men in Business: Essays in the Historical Role of the Entrepreneur* (New York: Harper & Row, 1962), pp. 254-285.

[56]P.D. Hall, "Social Foundations," pp. 109-110.

[57]On the origins of the social sciences at Harvard, see Paul Buck, ed., *The Social Sciences at Harvard, 1860-1920* (Cambridge: Harvard University Press, 1965).

[58]Harvard University, *Forty-Second Annual Report of the President of Harvard College for the Academical Year 1867-68* (Cambridge: Welch, Bigelow and Company, 1868), pp. 16-17.

[59]On Dunbar, see Robert L. Church, "The Economists Study Society: Sociology at Harvard, 1891-1902," Buck, *Social Sciences*, pp. 18-90; and Frank William Taussig, "Economics, 1871-1929" Morison, *Development of Harvard*, pp. 187-201.

[60]Sumner's connection to the Young Yale movement and to New York business interests is dealt with in detail in Harris E. Starr, *William Graham Sumner* (New York: Henry Holt & Company, 1925).

[61]On the role of the New York business community in the establishment of Columbia University's Faculty of Political Science, see. R. Gordon Hoxie, et al., *A History of the Faculty of Political Science Columbia University* (New York: Columbia University Press, 1955).

[62]On the ethical impulse in the establishment of the social sciences, see David B. Potts, "Social Ethics at Harvard, 1881-1931: A Study in Academic Activism," Buck, *Social Sciences*, pp. 91-128.

[63]At present there is no comprehensive examination of the philanthropic role of businessmen. Suggestive work in this area includes Heald, *Social Responsibilities*; Stuart Brandes, *American Welfare Capitalism, 1880-1940* (Chicago: University of Chicago Press, 1976); David Brody, *Workers in Industrial America* (New York: Oxford University Press, 1980); David F. Noble, *America by Design: Science, Technology, and the Rise of Corporate Capitalism* (New York: Oxford University Press, 1977); Louis Galambos, *Competition and Cooperation: The Emergence of a National Trade Association* (Baltimore: The Johns Hopkins University Press, 1966); and Ellis Hawley, ed., *Herbert Hoover as Secretary of Commerce: Studies in New Era Thought and Practice* (Iowa City: University of Iowa Press, 1981).

[64]Joseph Frazier Wall, *Andrew Carnegie* (New York: Oxford University Press, 1970), pp. 858-861.

[65]This account of the background to the establishment of the Russell Sage Foundation is based on Jane Smith's forthcoming *Commonwealth of Experts: Public Policy Research Institutions in the United States* (New York: Twentieth Century Fund, forthcoming). See also Barry D. Karl and Stanley N. Katz, "The American Private Philanthropic Foundation and the Public Sphere, 1890-1930," *Minerva*, vol. 19 (1981), pp. 236-270.

[66]Smith, *Commonwealth of Experts*, chapter two, pp. 14ff.

[67]*ibid.*, p. 15.

72   Peter Dobkin Hall

[68]For a succinct discussion of Hoover as an avatar of Big Government, see Paul Johnson, *Modern Times: The World from the Twenties to the Eighties* (New York: Harper & Row, 1983), pp. 241ff.

[69]The best account of the disintegration of the liberal policy establishment is Allen J. Matusow, *The Unraveling of America: A History of Liberalism in the 1960s* (New York: Harper & Row, 1984). Unfortunately, most of the accounts of "the establishment" (Mills, Domhoff, etc.) are crankish and partisan, based more on affiliational data than on an understanding of how the network of highly placed businessmen and professionals actually affected policy. One of the few careful examinations of the role of private universities, foundations, and elites in the policy process is John Stanfield's recently published *Philanthropy and Jim Crow in American Social Science* (Westport: Greenwood Press, 1984).

[70]Alan J. Abramson and Lester Salamon, *The Federal Budget and the Non-Profit Sector* (Washington: Urban Institute Press, 1982).

[71]Alan Pifer and Forrest Chisman, "Thinking about the Federal Social Role" (A Working Paper of the Project on the Federal Social Role, 1983). Another example of the new level of enquiry on which the role of the private sector is being explored is Robert L. Payton, *Major Challenges to Philanthropy* (Washington, DC: Independent Sector, 1984).